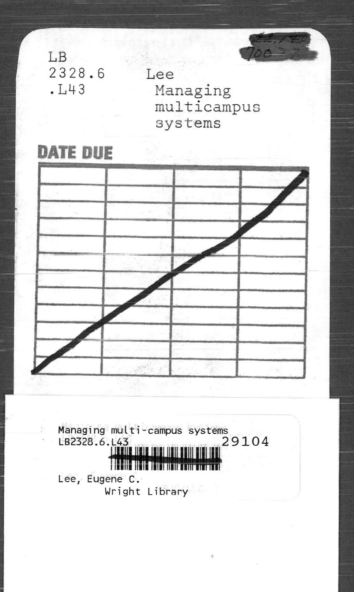

MANAGING
MULTICAMPUS
SYSTEMS

Effective Administration
in an Unsteady State

A REPORT FOR THE CARNEGIE COUNCIL
ON POLICY STUDIES IN HIGHER EDUCATION

Eugene C. Lee

Frank M. Bowen

MANAGING
MULTICAMPUS
SYSTEMS

Effective Administration
in an Unsteady State

Jossey-Bass Publishers
San Francisco · Washington · London · 1975

MANAGING MULTICAMPUS SYSTEMS
Effective Administration in an Unsteady State
by Eugene C. Lee and Frank M. Bowen

The Carnegie Council on Policy Studies in Higher Education,
2150 Shattuck Avenue, Berkeley, California 94704, has sponsored
preparation of this report as part of a continuing effort to
obtain and present significant information for public discussion.
The views expressed are those of the authors.

Copies are available from Jossey-Bass, San Francisco,
for the United States, Canada, and Possessions.
Copies for the rest of the world are available from
Jossey-Bass, London.

Library of Congress Catalogue Card Number LC 75-24012

International Standard Book Number ISBN 0-87589-264-7

Manufactured in the United States of America

DESIGN BY WILLI BAUM

FIRST EDITION

Code 7517

The Carnegie Council Series

The Federal Role in Postsecondary
Education: Unfinished Business,
1975-1980
*The Carnegie Council on Policy
Studies in Higher Education*

More than Survival: Prospects
for Higher Education in a
Period of Uncertainty
*The Carnegie Foundation for
the Advancement of Teaching*

Making Affirmative Action Work
in Higher Education: An Analysis
of Institutional and Federal
Policies with Recommendations
*The Carnegie Council on Policy
Studies in Higher Education*

Low or No Tuition: The Feasibil-
ity of a National Policy for the
First Two Years of College
*The Carnegie Council on Policy
Studies in Higher Education*

Managing Multicampus Systems:
Effective Administration in an
Unsteady State
Eugene C. Lee, Frank M. Bowen

Challenges Past, Challenges
Present: An Analysis of
American Higher Education
Since 1930
David D. Henry

Presidents Confront Reality:
From Edifice Complex to
University Without Walls
*Lyman A. Glenny, John R. Shea,
Janet H. Ruyle, Kathryn H. Freschi*

Contents

Foreword

Multicampus systems are among the most visible and influential institutions of higher education. Because most of them are public institutions, they interact closely with public policy-makers and are, consequently, highly sensitive to changes in the economic fortunes of our society and to shifting attitudes of our people. It is wise, therefore, when higher education generally finds itself in circumstances markedly different from those it had become accustomed to, to give multicampus institutions special attention.

We are in such a period now. After years of rapid enrollment growth and relatively abundant financial resources, higher education faces declining rates of enrollment and decreasing financial resources. It has become popular to refer to the new condition as the steady state because future changes in higher education must take place in the context of limited growth. The authors of this book, however, concentrate on the effects of the new situation on multicampus institutions and prefer to talk in terms of the unsteady state because they are impressed with the uneven impacts of general restraining factors on individual campuses within multicampus systems. On one campus enrollment growth continues, while on another it declines. Multicampus institutions therefore not only must respond to external conditions that affect them on a systemwide basis, but must also contend with internal disequilibria rooted in the diverse locations, program emphases, ages, traditions, and constituencies of the individual campuses. This internal disequilibrium keeps multicampus systems in an unsettled state even in the best of times. In times of stress, it complicates systemwide options and responses.

In theory, and to an extent in practice, the internal differences among campuses help these institutions survive in uncertain times. Young campuses can borrow prestige and stability from older ones; financially pressed campuses can receive help from those more abundantly endowed; faculty members whose following deserts them for more popular or more potentially rewarding offerings elsewhere have a better chance of being absorbed within a large system than on a single campus; and a single, prestigious voice in the state capitol may more easily command the attention of the legislature and governor than several smaller ones can.

The analysis provided by Eugene Lee and Frank Bowen demonstrates, however, that there are limitations to the ability of multicampus institutions to capitalize on these strengths. Students are not totally subject to institutional control. They cannot, for instance, be redirected from a popular to an unpopular campus solely for the good of the institution. The same is true of members of the faculty, who, even in times of shrinking academic employment opportunities, are to a considerable extent protected from unwanted relocation or from premature job termination by academic tradition, by tenure, and increasingly by collective bargaining. Resources cannot be freely allocated by the systemwide administration if financial control continues to drift away from them toward governors and statewide coordinating agencies.

The central lesson of the analysis provided by Lee and Bowen seems to be, therefore, that if multicampus systems are going to make the most of their unique advantages for survival and effectiveness, their flexibility must be considerable and needs to be protected. Such flexibility may be endangered by undue intrusions of state governments, by their own too highly bureaucratized central administration, by authority that is too widely dispersed and too absolute at the campus and department levels, or by the introduction of new coordinating centers with control over institutional procedures.

In this book, Lee and Bowen provide us with an informative and useful sequel to *The Multicampus University* (1971), which they prepared under the sponsorship of the Carnegie Commission on Higher Education. We are pleased that they have given the benefit of their extensive experience in university, government, and state financial affairs to this new study for the Carnegie Council on Policy Studies in Higher Education.

Clark Kerr
Chairman
Carnegie Council on Policy
Studies in Higher Education

Preface

Higher education in the United States faces an uncertain future. Still affected by public disapproval of past campus unrest, buffeted by economic inflation and recession, it confronts the bleak prospect of enrollment stabilization or decline over the coming decade. The broad parameters of this uncertain future with its perils and opportunities are the topic of *More Than Survival*, a cautiously optimistic commentary by the Carnegie Foundation for the Advancement of Teaching (1975). *Managing Multicampus Systems* is one of four reports commissioned by the Carnegie Foundation in early 1974 to provide background for its commentary.[1] In it, we describe and evaluate the experiences of nine multicampus systems in coping with and planning for a period of limited growth, fiscal constraints, and possible retrenchment.

Aside from a brief description of each system in Chapter One and introductory comments to other chapters, this is not a conscious updating of our comprehensive earlier work, *The Multicampus University* (1971). While we deal with the same nine multicampus systems as in 1971—the Universities of California, Illinois, Missouri, North Carolina, Texas, Wisconsin, the City and State Universities of New York, and the California

[1]The three other studies commissioned by the Carnegie Foundation are a study of enrollment projections until the year 2000 (Carlson and Gordon, 1975), a national survey of the experiences and expectations of institutional presidents (Glenny and others, 1975), and a historical review of changes in higher education since 1930 (Henry, 1975).

State Universities and Colleges—we concentrate here on academic affairs, budgeting, student admissions and transfers, and faculty staffing, all specifically within the context of multicampus governance.

Although narrower in purpose, the current study has wider applicability than did the earlier volume. The term *multicampus university,* as defined in the earlier study, covered only eleven systems, nine of which were investigated. At least five other institutions now fit that definition. Moreover, legislative restructuring changed two systems so that they are no longer covered by that definition, which excluded the so-called single board states. Now, the Universities of North Carolina and Wisconsin are statewide governing boards for all senior public colleges and universities, a form of coordination and governance found in 18 other states. In addition, there is a growing variety of multicampus systems other than those here discussed—for example, those in which the system executive continues as the head of the main campus, those where campus executives report directly to the board, and those which involve two or more community college campuses. Distinctions among various types of multicampus systems are critical, but major internal issues are common to each, and we believe this study speaks to them.

Information for *Managing Multicampus Systems* was gathered in much the same way as that for our earlier study: by reviewing pertinent documents and interviewing the system chief executive officers and their central administrative staffs. The major difference—an extremely important one—is that time limitations prohibited interviews with campus administrators and faculty. We know that campuses are where the action is. This book therefore is not a final evaluation of multicampus success or failure. It could not be such an evaluation in any case because the conditions limiting growth are recent. In most instances, multicampus responses are in their formative and initial stages; only rarely have they been in effect long enough to have had measurable impact on the individual institutions. We did informally collect opinions from campus administrators and faculty about individual campus activities, and some of their opinions are mentioned in the book. In general, however, our information comes from systemwide administrators.

The study began in early 1974, when we sent a questionnaire to the chief executive officer of each of the nine multicampus universities. The questionnaire was designed to help us select major and relatively common areas of concern. The questionnaire (summarized at the back of the book) was neither developed nor intended as an independent research instrument. Responses were aggregated and reported to each system in mid-1974, before interviews were undertaken.

In the early summer, two or three days were spent at each system interviewing central administrative staff. In all, more than 100 persons were interviewed. Subsequently, drafts of substantive chapters (Chapters Two through Seven) were completed and mailed to each system for review. Comments were received from all, and these were often integrated into the text and utilized in the development of our conclusions (Chapter Eight). Telephone interviews were used to clarify specific points as the final draft was prepared in the spring of 1975.

By design and not oversight, several important areas of multicampus governance are not dealt with here, despite their obvious importance. Among these are education in the health sciences, libraries, centralized computer services, and affirmative action. High on systemwide agendas, they demand specialized treatment.

We introduce the nine multicampus universities in Chapter One, with a brief history of each and a short comment on changes in governance since the earlier study. In Chapter Two, we describe the differing emphases of formal systemwide academic plans and the increased planning activity now taking place. The growing comprehensiveness and stringency of systemwide review of new academic programs and the establishment of procedures for review of existing programs are the topics of Chapter Three. Chapter Four discusses budgeting, particularly enrollment-driven formulas and system flexibility. Attempts to stretch resources through innovative academic programs such as nontraditional and multicampus offerings are explored in Chapter Five. The impact of prospective and actual retrenchment on faculty is considered in Chapter Six, and its impact on student admissions and transfers is discussed in Chapter Seven. In Chapter Eight, we draw conclusions from the experiences of the nine multicampus systems and attempt to chart the directions in which they must move to meet the challenge of the 1980s, the challenge of the unsteady state.

Acknowledgments

Higher education in general and multicampus systems in particular stand at a critical point in time. We offer some guideposts for decision and action here with respect and admiration for those who must make those decisions and bear responsibility for their consequences. We write in the hope that our efforts may, in some small measure, match the dedication and commitment to higher education which it has been our privilege to observe and report here.

For assistance in the preparation of this book, we are indebted to more people than can be briefly named. The major contributors have been the multicampus chief executive officers themselves: Chancellors Ernest Boyer, Glenn Dumke, Robert Kibbee, and Charles LeMaistre, and Presidents John Corbally, William Friday, Charles Hitch, Brice Ratchford, and John Weaver. The study simply would not have been possible without their generosity in time and their candor in discussion. Their unfailing hospitality and that of their staffs made each visit professionally rewarding and personally enjoyable. We are particularly grateful to the individuals in each system who arranged our visits and to the more than 100 staff members whom we interviewed and whose contributions provide the basis for much of the book. The contributions of other systemwide staff are less apparent but equally real: they furnished extensive documentation, answered our lengthy preliminary questionnaire, helped us understand enrollment trends, and provided other essential background information.

Organizational and secretarial tasks increase geometrically with the number of authors, as Denise Fynmore, Rose Hill, Nancy Kuriloff, Catherine Winter, and Marsha Wagner discovered. So do editorial responsibilities, as Verne Stadtman, associate director of the Carnegie Council, was well aware from our earlier study. The second line of editorial defense for the present book was manned by JB Hefferlin at Jossey-Bass. We thank them all, not only for their help, but for their patience.

None of these people would have been involved if it had not been for the support of the Carnegie Council on Policy Studies in Higher Education and its chairman, Clark Kerr. Generous assistance was available when needed, and wise counsel was offered when requested. No more could be desired, and we are deeply grateful.

Berkeley, California   Eugene C. Lee
September 1975   Frank M. Bowen

MANAGING
MULTICAMPUS
SYSTEMS
Effective Administration in an Unsteady State

A REPORT FOR THE CARNEGIE COUNCIL
ON POLICY STUDIES IN HIGHER EDUCATION

1

The Unsteady State of Multicampus Systems: Context and Governance

These are troubled times for higher education. Hiring of faculty is frozen at the University of Missouri, a drastic reduction is proposed in the current operating budget of the City University of New York, and in Wisconsin a gubernatorial directive requires the university to plan for phasing out and phasing down campuses and programs.

But the news is not all bad. To varying degrees these three multicampus systems and the other six which we first studied five years ago (Lee and Bowen, 1971)—the Universities of California, Illinois, North Carolina, and Texas, the California State University and Colleges, and the State University of New York—have realized the potential of a structure in which the whole can become greater than the sum of its parts. Systemwide academic planning and review of new and existing programs are less isolated from budgetary processes, and all three are beginning to address the issue of faculty recruitment and renewal in a period of academic personnel stability. If dollars are short, initiative is long, and instructional programs now cross campus boundaries more often than they did in 1970.

Fiscal stringency, inflation, enrollment stabilization, and social changes since 1970 have had differing impact on the nine systems, and their responses have been equally varied. These patterns of multicampus impact and response are the subject of this report.

The Unsteady State

History is unlikely to relegate either the past five years or the next ten to obscurity. As a nation, we are now painfully aware that our economy is both fragile and dependent on the rest of the world. Inflation and energy shortages turn fixed costs to spiraling ones; fixed income becomes declining income. For higher education, the shock of national economic dislocation is compounded by the recognition of more specific difficulties. Dwindling lines of applicants for admission are expected to grow even shorter. Job markets for recent graduates, teachers, and holders of some advanced degrees are shrinking. For faculty, tenure still protects academic freedom, but it may not ensure job security so much as a fair hearing before the position is phased out.

Recent years have brought other changes to higher education which, if less dramatic, are no less far-reaching. Lowering of the voting age to 18 years has given impetus to an already aroused student interest in university governance. Higher education is now called *postsecondary education,* a term that recognizes the expanded role of proprietary schools and other alternatives to traditional colleges and universities. While the latter have not been transformed into the political instruments for social change earlier demanded, the institutions are now more sensitive to the needs and demands of the public and its political representatives.

The slowing rate of enrollment is the most publicized aspect of this new environment. Although some institutions are still expanding, the national growth rate has declined with wide variation among individual states. The seven states in the present study reflect this variation. Whereas higher education enrollment for the nation as a whole increased by 18 percent between 1970 and 1974, four of the seven exceeded this figure—North Carolina (30 percent), Texas (24 percent), California (22 percent) and New York (18.4 percent); three fell below—Illinois

(17.9 percent), Wisconsin (13 percent) and Missouri (8 percent) (The Carnegie Foundation for the Advancement of Teaching, 1975).

National enrollment expectations also vary widely. A report of The Carnegie Foundation for the Advancement of Teaching (1975) discusses the varying assumptions behind different projections: a declining rate of growth until the early 1980s, stable enrollment or perhaps absolute declines from then until 1995, but growth thereafter until the year 2000, although at a slower rate than at present (The Carnegie Foundation, 1975).

Today, administrators in all nine multicampus systems are challenged by growth inhibiting factors which have emerged in the past five years and are expected in the next. Shrinking financial support and stabilizing enrollment, the major inhibitions to physical growth, encompass a more complex set of variables. If a single factor such as enrollment is isolated, the appearance of a steady state may seem likely. But the isolation of one factor does not capture the current reality of multicampus governance.

To the contrary. These nine multicampus systems face an increasingly unsteady state of uneven and unpredictable distribution of students across campuses, with corresponding uncertainty in state and federal support. Differential enrollment and support—deliberately planned and otherwise—have always been a part of the multicampus scene, but in 1975 the problems these factors raise have dramatically increased in intensity. Constant or steady enrollment for the system as a whole almost always entails growth at one campus and decline at another. The result is generally imbalance, never steadiness, and often turbulence described in at least one system as "street warfare."

Why Study Multicampus Systems?

Enrollment at the nine multicampus universities in our study comprises approximately 25 percent of all students in public four-year colleges and universities in the United States. Size alone justifies a close look at their experiences and responses. More importantly, these nine institutions are *systems* which both govern *and* coordinate several campuses. Authority of their central administrations for academic affairs is insulated from day-to-day campus pressures but coupled, nevertheless, with operational responsibilities. Kenneth Boulding (1974) notes that the larger the organization, the more likely it is to adjust successfully during a period of decline. He is concerned, however, that adjustment may be at the expense of smaller institutions and entail a loss of variety. He also cautions that large institutions may lack internal flexibility.

In a period of inhibited growth, therefore, multicampus systems have the advantage of size and the added benefit of a form of governance with potential for variety and change. Even with fewer students and less support, a multicampus system can maintain its effectiveness by pursuing the objectives of campus diversity, where the system promotes different academic and administrative approaches at different campuses; campus specialization, where different goals are designated for different campuses; and campus cooperation where academic resources are shared by several campuses. These objectives, desirable during a period of growth, may become necessary conditions of survival as enrollment stabilizes for all multicampus systems, including university and senior college systems and the increasing number of community college districts with more than one campus.

Nine Multicampus Universities

Each of the nine multicampus systems is the product of its own history and of the particular political, social, and economic environment of its state. This section briefly compares findings from our earlier study and the current status of each institution. Enrollment trends and projections included here afford perspective for subsequent chapters. Of greater importance, however, the information portrays the uneven distribution of enrollment among the campuses within each system. This differential impact compounds the problem of enrollment stabilization or decline where it exists, as in the University of Wisconsin, and anticipates it elsewhere, as in the Universities of Illinois and Texas.

In general, the older, more well-established university campuses have been less affected by enrollment stabilization or decline than more recent additions to university rank and comprehensive colleges. Nationally, public institutions classified by the Office of Education as universities increased their total enrollment by 5.8 percent compared to 3.9 percent for other four-year institutions in the two-year period, 1972-1974. Full-time enrollments for the same two-year period show a greater contrast: a 5.4 percent growth for universities and a 1.0 decline for other four-year institutions. On the other hand, for the single-year period, 1973-1974, other four-year institutions showed greater percentage growth of full-time enrollments than did universities—2.1 percent compared to 0.9 percent even though this greater growth did not offset the earlier absolute decline ("Opening Fall Enrollments 1972, 1973, and 1974," 1974).

Student preference for long established institutions is a relevant factor in virtually all of the nine multicampus systems in this study. Undergraduates seek a better education (or a more impressive degree) from such campuses as Chapel Hill or Madison in preference to lesser known schools. Moreover, the continued high participation rate of highly motivated and qualified undergraduates who anticipate graduate or professional education and are attracted to the established campuses may offset demographic decreases and dampened participation in the overall applicant pool. More prestigious university campuses do, however, share some part of the financial distress of less fortunate campuses in the same system. This has already happened in the Universities of California, Missouri, and Wisconsin.

California State University and Colleges. The 14 campuses of California State Colleges were united by the California Master Plan legislation of 1960 under a single board and separate system executive, designated chancellor. Despite state fiscal constraints, the separate campuses were headed by strong and relatively autonomous campus executives, designated presidents. Although the level of state control was modified, giving greater authority to the board and the system executive, a high degree of state supervision remained at the time of our 1971 study, when the number of campuses had increased to 19. Several of the campuses are comparable to many universities in size and qualifications of faculty and students, but under the California Master Plan these campuses cannot award doctoral degrees on their own.

In 1971, the name of the California State Colleges was legislatively changed to the California State University and Colleges. The change of name was not intended to alter the primary undergraduate mission of the system, nor has it. The state has continued to relax fiscal controls, but—in contrast to the University of California, with its constitutional status—the system is still described as a "creature of the legislature." Although the 19 campuses have parallel missions, some draw students from throughout California and from other states, while others are primarily regional.

For the system as a whole, annual full-time enrollment increased from 181,254 in 1969-70 to 218,134 in 1973-74, the latter figure being virtually identical to a 1968 projection of 217,670. For some individual campuses, however, the projections were wide of the mark. In 1968, for example, enrollment at the Hayward campus—then 6,675—was projected at 12,440 in 1973-74. Actual enrollment in 1973-74, however, was 8,905 after three successive years of decline. Well located, staffed, and administered, the relatively new Hayward campus lacks an image that is competitive with others in the San Francisco Bay Area. In contrast, distinctive campuses such as Humboldt and Sonoma grew beyond projected enrollment during the same period, despite their rural locations.

Currently, as systemwide growth rates have dropped from 10 percent annually to 2 percent, long range enrollment projections have been drastically reduced: "While the system is still growing, the cumulative reductions of the last five annual long range reallocations now stands at 93,630. That is, in 1970, we forecast 354,630 FTE [full-time enrollment] for 1980-81; we now have set that figure at 261,000. In effect we have eliminated the equivalent of 10 [campuses the size of the campus at Pomona] from our future" (California State University and Colleges, 1973a).

In 1974, the projection of 261,000 for 1980-81 was re-

duced to 247,100. The dramatic lowering of full-time enrollment projections is not attributable to earlier neglect of demographic trends. Projected numbers of students are showing up at
the campuses, but large numbers of them are increasingly taking
fewer courses. Although the system has always had many part-
time students, the current situation prompted one administrator
to state that "there is no such thing as a full-time student any
longer—all of them are attempting less work." It is possible that
more students are supporting themselves through outside employment and feel less urgency to leave school. Regardless of
the reason, relatively minor changes in average student credit
units has a major impact on earlier projections when applied to
200,000 students.

Like the University of California, the State University is
uncertain of the role of the newly created California Postsecondary Education Commission, the successor to the previous
coordinating agency.

University of California. Early in its history, the flagship campus—Berkeley—established specialized medical and agricultural
branches; a two-year branch of the university in Los Angeles soon
became a separate four-year and graduate institution; other
campuses were established around specialized activities (for
example, San Diego around the Scripps Oceanographic Research
Station), built from the ground up (Santa Cruz), or acquired
from the state college system (Santa Barbara). The pattern of a
decentralized multicampus system did not develop until the late
1950s, signaled by the use of the title chancellor for campus
executives. At the time of our first study, there were nine campuses and no immediate plans for expansion.

Today, the University of California gives little appearance
of organizational change, but changes have in fact taken place.
Enrollment constraints limit aspirations of newer campuses to
achieve the status of Berkeley and UCLA. These two are now at
centrally imposed enrollment ceilings, and the Davis campus is
expected to reach its ceiling by 1976.

Full-time-equivalent enrollment increased for the system as
a whole from 98,495 in 1969-70 to 111,764 in 1973-74, sub-

stantially short of the 1969 projection of 123,970. The shortfall is unevenly distributed across campuses, with the Riverside campus being particularly hard pressed to recruit to capacity. Riverside's difficulties are in part attributable to smog drifting east from Los Angeles, but also—in circular fashion—to pervasive uncertainty over campus objectives in the face of enrollment difficulties. Long range projections for the system in 1974 indicate slowing growth through 1982-83, again with major impact on smaller campuses. Since 1969, for example, expected headcount enrollment for the eight general campuses in 1978 has been lowered from 133,531 to 114,531, but four campuses—Santa Cruz, Santa Barbara, Irvine, and Riverside—bear the brunt of this decline.

As new campuses were established during the 1960s, faculty were recruited under the assumption that enrollments would increase sufficiently to support a wide range of advanced graduate programs. The assumption is no longer justified, and the University of California shares with the University of Missouri the problem of allocating resources among several campuses all of which offer doctoral programs. In both systems, expectations of many campus faculty and administrators are undergoing radical change.

The system also shares with the University of Missouri and the California State University and Colleges the existence of a new and as yet untried coordinating agency.

University of Illinois. Besides the flagship campus at Urbana, the University of Illinois early established a separate medical center in Chicago, headed first by an executive dean and then by a vice-president. In 1965, the undergraduate program, first established in Chicago following World War II, developed into the Chicago Circle campus. Campus executives in Chicago and Urbana were given the title of chancellor during the years 1966 to 1968, and administrative services were reorganized accordingly.

The three-campus University of Illinois has the fewest campuses of the systems in the study. Urbana remains the predominant public institution offering advanced graduate work in Illinois. It has grown slightly, while maintaining selective admission policies during recent years. During the same period, its one-time rival, Southern Illinois University, has suffered substantial and well publicized enrollment shortfalls. Of the nine systems in the study, the University of Illinois appears least disturbed by current enrollment trends.

Between 1969 and 1974, opening fall headcount enrollment increased from 51,926 to 58,749 for the system as a whole, short of a 1970 projection of 63,957. Growth of the Chicago Circle campus has been substantially less than projected: 19,393 in fall 1974 in contrast to the 1970 projection of 23,300. In part, this shortfall may be attributable to the overly optimistic expectation of the statewide master plan that the percentage of college-age youth enrolled at all campuses in the state would increase from 60 to 68 percent during this period. In fact, the percentage has remained constant. In addition, Chicago Circle has fallen below projections for more complex reasons: inability to obtain coordinating agency approval for needed graduate programs, an innercity location, and competition from other Chicago-area campuses, public and private, in part-time instruction. University projections in 1974 indicate relatively constant enrollment over the next ten years, with the major campus at Urbana remaining stable because of enrollment ceilings initiated by the campus and endorsed by the system administration.

University of Missouri. For many years, the flagship campus at Columbia included a specialized engineering school, Rolla, which was geographically separated from the main campus although organizationally part of it. In 1963, a new campus in St. Louis was developed out of a former two-year college and the private University of Kansas City was acquired. By 1964, the office of president, freed from all direct campus operating responsibilities, was established and the executives of all four campuses were given the title of chancellor.

Currently, the University of Missouri has the same campuses, and the same problems with their locations, as it had in 1971, the time of our first study. The major campus at Columbia is located in the center of the state, midway between St. Louis and Kansas City. Although the broad range of Columbia's graduate programs gives it national stature, the two newer campuses in urban population areas have developed specific graduate programs which are perceived by some to be both competitive and superior to those at Columbia.

Overall, the system grew from an opening fall headcount enrollment of 45,251 in 1969 to 49,520 in 1974, well short of the 1969 projection of 60,409. During this period, the Rolla campus actually dropped in enrollment from 5,235 to 4,064 in contrast to the 1969 projection of 7,127. With its specialization in engineering and physics (and an isolated rural location), the Rolla campus was particularly susceptible to the nationwide lack of student demand for such programs.

A dramatic lowering of enrollment expectations is particularly evident in Missouri, which now projects a virtually static pattern. The 1978 projection of 69,907, made in 1969 for the system as a whole, was revised downward in 1974 to 51,735. By 1985, absolute enrollment declines are expected at all campuses. At the St. Louis campus in particular, faculty recruited under the earlier assumption that enrollment growth would support advanced graduate programs face the same adjustment problems as their counterparts at some of the newer campuses of the University of California.

Like both California systems, the University of Missouri is working with a new coordinating agency.

City University of New York. Originally, both City College and Hunter College were under the city Board of Education, and then had separate boards, which in 1926 were merged into the Board of Higher Education. In 1961, the name was changed to City University and authority to award doctoral degrees was given. By 1969, the campuses of City College, Hunter, Brooklyn, and Queens were joined by six other four-year and six two-year campuses. In addition, a unique, physically separate, systemwide graduate center and an affiliated medical school were introduced. Campus executives (presidents), paramount before appointment of a separate system executive (chancellor) in 1960, must now share authority with that official.

The City University of New York is now a dramatically different institution than in 1970. Two more community colleges have been added, and the governing board has been reorganized to permit appointments by the governor as well as by the mayor.

However, the most significant change is the open-admissions policy, implemented in 1970, which has greatly increased both the size of the possible applicant pool and the diversity among applicants. Open admissions also makes earlier enrollment projections virtually meaningless. For example, the number of first-time freshmen increased by over 15,000 students in the first years of the program; at the four-year campuses, head-count enrollment grew from 113,213 in fall 1969 to 168,871 in fall 1974; enrollment at the community colleges increased from 47,654 to 84,366. Although increased enrollments were projected through 1980 as recently as 1972, current projections are for a slight overall decrease between 1975 and 1980.

The current major objective of City University—absorbing and distributing the new students brought in through open admissions—is compounded by the fiscal difficulties of the city of New York. Among the nine systems in the study, City University, along with the University of Wisconsin, faces the most severe fiscal pressure. In the City University system, however, the impact is unrelated to enrollment declines.

State University of New York. The State University of New York is responsible for all public education outside the city system. Some elements of the governance of the State University, therefore, are more associated with single board states than with multicampus structures constituting only a part of all state higher education. Several two- and four-year campuses (none a university) were placed under a new board in 1948, headed by a system executive, designated chancellor. At the time of our first study in 1971, the State University totalled 30 campuses: four either at or approaching university status, 11 four-year liberal arts campuses, two medical centers, seven specialized professional schools, and six two-year colleges. The State University also had limited supervisory authority over 31 state-operated two-year colleges.

Today, the State University of New York has direct governing authority over 34 state-operated campuses, three more than in 1970. One of these, Empire State College, was established in 1971 to offer degrees to part-time students for off-campus work, and is a significant change both structurally and academically.

The fall headcount enrollment of the campuses directly governed by the State University grew from 136,721 in 1969 to 189,450 in 1974, substantially less than a 1968 projection of 213,205 and a 1972 projection of 191,898. The 1972 projection was based on the assumption that the college-going rate for New York high school graduates would increase throughout the 1970s from 66 percent in 1971 to 75 percent in 1980. In fact, the rate declined to 65 percent in 1972 and 63 percent in 1973. While the system as a whole will continue to grow, long term projections are being substantially revised. In early 1975, it was suggested that the 1980 projection of 248,031 made three years earlier be lowered by some 20,000. Between 1980 and 1990, the state education department projects relatively stable enrollment in the university centers but a decline of over 30 percent in the four-year state college campuses.

To date, the impact of enrollment trends has been fairly evenly distributed across State University campuses. Concern at the newer university centers, Albany and Binghamton, however, is similar to that at the newer campuses of the Universities of California and Missouri: enrollment may not be sufficient to support the range of advanced graduate programs that were an integral part of campus plans.

University of North Carolina. The depression forced the shotgun wedding of previously independent campuses at Chapel Hill, Greensboro, and Raleigh into the University of North Carolina in 1931, with each campus headed by a vice-president, a title changed in 1945 to chancellor. By 1971, three more campuses had been added. Our earlier study noted the minimal central administration of this system—significant funding decisions were often negotiated directly between the campuses and the state—and the university was described as a "loose confederation held together by the legislative budget committee."

Shotgun weddings have not gone out of style in North Carolina, at least to bring together institutions of higher education. Legislation in 1971 merged ten previously independent public campuses with the six-campus University of North Carolina. A new governing board was created, but local campus boards with limited powers continue. Legislation also freed the system from much of the detailed state budgetary control that distinguished it from the other multicampus systems in 1970.

Overall, the fall opening enrollment headcount of the 16 institutions grew from 74,111 in 1969 to 97,031 in fall 1974, at substantially the rate projected by the coordinating agency in 1968. Enrollment of six campuses, however, has declined since 1972, although only one did not increase enrollment in fall 1974 over fall 1973. Current long range projections are for continued moderate growth until 1980 followed by stabilization or moderate decline from 1980 to 1990. Planning in North Carolina will be influenced by the terms of the desegregation plan of the state, in agreement with the federal Department of Health, Education and Welfare (HEW), which requires that the five predominantly black campuses be maintained and strengthened.

University of Texas. In addition to the flagship campus at Austin, the university for many years maintained several medical and health branches. In 1913, the system expanded to include the El Paso campus (originally a mining college, now a general academic institution) and in 1965 the Arlington campus (acquired from the Texas A & M system). In 1969, the legislature authorized the university to establish seven new units: a general four-year campus, two upper-division campuses, and four schools in the health professions.

Today, the University of Texas stands in direct contrast to the other multicampus systems in the study. Instead of consolidating in the face of stabilizing or declining enrollments, the University of Texas is growing. The number of general campuses has recently doubled—from three to six—with the addition of a four-year campus in San Antonio and two upper-division campuses, one in Dallas and the other, Permian Basin, in Odessa.

The systemwide fall headcount enrollment grew from 60,032 at the three general campuses in 1969 to 72,365 at the six campuses in 1974. Growth at the Arlington and El Paso campuses, however, has fallen short of projections made in 1968 by the coordinating agency. By 1980, overall enrollment at the six campuses is projected at 111,085, with over 32,000 of that growth attributable to the three new campuses. Although continued growth through 1990 is projected for all but the El Paso campus, some doubts have been expressed concerning the validity of these estimates.

University of Wisconsin. The flagship campus at Madison was joined after World War I by numerous lower-division, two-year branches. The Milwaukee campus was acquired in 1956 from the state college system. In 1964, the title of chancellor was given to executives of both four-year campuses as well as to the executive of the two-year center system. Six of the two-year centers were merged into two four-year campuses in 1971.

Legislation in 1971 directed the consolidation of the University of Wisconsin and the Wisconsin State University System, but final details of the merger were not enacted until 1974. At present, the system consists of 13 senior and 14 two-year campuses. Of the 13 senior campuses, Madison and Milwaukee—the doctoral cluster—offer advanced graduate instruction. The remaining senior campuses—the university cluster—offer baccalaureate and selected graduate work below the doctoral level, and two of these have special missions, Green Bay in environmental studies and Stout in professional and technical education.

Opening fall enrollment of the system grew from 127,147 in 1969 to 139,891 in 1974, substantially short of the 160,187 projected by the coordinating agency in 1969. Absolute enrollment declines at several campuses in 1973-74 were reflected in budgetary reductions required by an inflexible statutory funding formula. In addition, a gubernatorially mandated "productivity savings" requirement reduced the budget base of the system for the 1973-75 biennium by 7.5 percent—some $21.5 million. As a result, over 500 probationary faculty contracts were not renewed, and 88 tenured faculty and staff were given notice of layoff. The option of reducing faculty positions through attrition was not available to the University of Wisconsin as it had been to the Universities of California and Missouri.

Long-term projections have been revised downward. The 1969 projection of 177,981 in 1980 was reduced in 1973 to 150,708. Enrollment is expected to decline at all campuses after 1980. The trauma of actual faculty layoffs gives greater urgency to enrollment-related systemwide academic planning than appears in any other system, with the possible exception of the University of Missouri.

Governance by State Agencies

The present report does not describe either the governing structures of multicampus systems or their relationships with state governmental and coordinating agencies as separate, major topics. Recent developments are summarized here.

Executive and legislative agencies. Governors and their staffs remain the major focus of state governmental influence on higher education in all nine multicampus systems. In Illinois, this influence increased in 1971 when a constitutional amendment gave the governor budgetary line-item veto authority. In New York, on the other hand, while the governor's formal budgetary authority remains the same, the legislature appears increasingly assertive since the retirement of Nelson Rockefeller. If California is representative, the Democratic gubernatorial victories in 1974 will result in little if any additional financial support for higher education.

Legislative changes have been largely in the direction of increasing staff assistance. Together with the executive budget office, legislative fiscal committees are being staffed by recent holders of advanced degrees in political science, economics, and public administration. One system administrator considers this a mixed blessing. While pleased that state government makes more use of academically trained professionals—many from his own university—he is concerned that these recent graduates lack desired experience with higher education and, importantly, do not always recognize or accept the difference between the university and other state agencies.

Coordinating agencies. The major impact of statewide coordinating agencies is their exercise of authority over academic programs. At the Universities of Illinois and Texas, some joint academic programs across campuses reflect actual or anticipated coordinating agency refusal to approve a new single-campus program judged to be unnecessarily duplicative. New programs at the City and State Universities of New York are also subject to intensive review by the coordinating agency, the Regents of the University of the State of New York. For the two New York systems, however, a structured review of existing doctoral programs across both public and private campuses is having the greater immediate impact ("Statewide Planning vs. University Autonomy," 1975). The restructured coordinating agencies in California and Missouri are expected to emphasize academic program review. The seven multicampus systems in these five states continue to face an old issue: What is the proper role of a coordinating agency in academic program review of the multicampus system? Lanier (1973), for example, discusses this issue in the context of the relationship between the University of Illinois and the Illinois Board of Higher Education.

The shape of statewide coordination will differ in the future because of the still uncertain scope of statewide planning activity required of "1202 Commissions" by the Federal Higher Education Act of 1972. Major statewide academic program issues will (and in a pluralistic society, probably should) continue to be sources of tension. But the task of planning for all postsecondary education, the major charge of the commissions, is a demanding one. Issues of primarily internal interest to multicampus systems may be more easily resolved in the future as other critical priorities take precedence in the broader planning context. At least, many hope so.

Internal Governance and Administration

Governing boards. Both composition and operation of the multicampus governing boards have recently changed in several states. In North Carolina and Wisconsin, new boards govern the legislatively merged statewide systems. In the City University of New York, gubernatorial appointees now sit on the governing board, in addition to appointees of the mayor. In the University of California, a constitutional amendment in 1974 reduced the terms of board members from 16 years to 12 and changed the composition of ex officio membership permitting, although not requiring, student and faculty members.

Relations between the central administrative staff and their boards have improved in the past five years. When student disorder was the issue of the day in the late 1960s, board members tended to be outsiders reacting with the general public. Now, as is particularly evident in Missouri and Wisconsin, fiscal stringency has made board members insiders supportive of administrative and faculty efforts.

Central administration. In 1975, three of the multicampus chief executive officers held the same position they did five years earlier. In three other systems, persons who were senior staff members at the time of our earlier study held the higher executive position, one of these (at the University of Missouri) filling the vacancy created by the lateral move of the chief executive to another system in the study (the University of Wisconsin). Despite the changing personalities in all systems, the general organization of the central administrative staffs changed little over the five-year period.

However, our earlier prediction (1971, pp. 143-144) of an increasing role in multicampus administration for the chief executive's prestigious chief deputy may have been in error. In two systems, the position did not survive retirement of the incumbent, and is now held by two senior staff officers with somewhat overlapping responsibilities, whose relationship to the system chief executive is described as a team approach.

Faculty. Changes in the structure or role of the organized faculty in systemwide governance have not been substantial. An increased role for faculty senates is reported in only two systems—the California State University and Colleges and the University of North Carolina. In two others, the City and State Universities of New York, systemwide faculty organizations have held their own in retaining influence over academic affairs as opposed to the "bread and butter" issues negotiated by collective bargaining agents. On the other hand, at the University of Wisconsin a strong tradition of campus autonomy and the complexities of possible collective bargaining legislation are delaying and may prevent the establishment of a systemwide faculty organization. None of the system chief executives expects the role of a systemwide faculty organization to increase in the future, in some instances because of collective bargaining. This trend is unfortunate, for future systemwide reallocations will benefit from broad faculty participation and influence. In the University of California, for example, a committee of the systemwide senate recommends a very active faculty role in program review and resource allocation (University of California, 1975a).

Student organizations. The number of multicampus systems with systemwide student organizations increased from four to six in the past five years and, in the opinion of systemwide administrators in five of these, the role of students in governance also increased. More evident, however, is the greater influence students now have in state capitals. In New York, the legislative newsletter of the State University student lobby is a resource used by other lobbyists. In the City University, the student senate led a group of nearly 10,000 marchers to the City Hall in early 1975 to protest a proposed budget reduction. In California, the student lobby is one of the 20 most effective lobbying organizations, according to a poll of state legislators.

Single governing boards. Neither the complex origins nor the still developing results of mergers in North Carolina and Wisconsin are explored in detail here except as these issues relate to current enrollment and fiscal trends. However, with the advantage of having seen the two systems before and after merger—albeit at a highly general level—we can venture some impressions. We do so, at least in part, because our views differ substantially from those offered by Harold Enarson, President of Ohio State University, in a well-publicized commencement address in 1973: "In both states, the state colleges and universities have been formally merged into a single, new, all-embracing state university. It is a triumph of system—a new empire, a new total bureaucracy" (Enarson, 1973).

Enarson put forward three reasons for this "triumph of system": the impulse of government itself to extend its domain and control, the rapid movement toward the development of powerful state systems of higher education, and excessive reliance on management development tools. Perhaps. But we suggest that the two mergers are attributable less to the actions, deliberate or otherwise, of bureaucrats, coordinators, and systems analysts than to the consequences of allowing institutional disputes to drift into the arena of state politics.

As for the results, one can neither celebrate nor condemn a "triumph of system" without examining its details, and it may be too soon for evaluation in any event. Assuredly both systems must walk a narrow path to maintain balance among the diverse dimensions of quality present in individual campuses. But the State University of New York is, we believe, an example of another large system in which this path has already been followed successfully.

The combination of governing and coordinating authority in a multicampus system allows resource allocation among campuses by academicians—or at least by academic administrators. At the University of North Carolina, for example, a phased four-year program for library improvement benefits all campuses while recognizing differences among them. In Wisconsin, merger allows shifting of funds and faculty among campuses to ease the impact of uneven realization of enrollment expectations. In the absence of a multicampus system structure, these actions might have resulted from decisions by state executive and legislative offices or by a coordinating agency. And however able coordinating agency staff may be, and whatever academic qualifications they may have, they do not, in the words of a system administrator, "have to come in on Monday morning to live with the decisions they made on Friday."

2

Academic Planning

The academic plan is a basic instrument of multicampus governance. It is here that aspirations of several campuses are brought together and articulated, redundant programs eliminated, program gaps remedied, and the whole made greater than the sum of the parts. In academic plans, system executives and governing boards look at the total system in the context of the needs and expectations of society. In a period of limited growth, such plans take on added significance—or should. Confronted with resource scarcity, priorities are no longer simply desirable but essential.

That is the theory. Reality is often different. Internal and external forces operate sharply to modify academic plans, even as they are adopted. But decisions must be made, buildings designed, programs approved, and budgets allocated. Can academic planning improve the quality of these decisions in an uncertain future? What are the barriers to the effectiveness and implementation of academic plans?

Academic planning in the nine multicampus systems has changed dramatically—and for the better—since our earlier study. At that time, we found (Lee and Bowen, 1971, pp. 228-229, 233):

> Within the nine multicampus universities, *formal* documentary evidence of academic planning is absent

as much as it is present. In only four states are the university systems required to prepare formal academic plans. . . .

The potential [for effective planning] is there, but it requires an assertion of universitywide academic leadership vis-à-vis the campuses that has not yet been accepted at either campus or system levels. If the system is to be more than a collection of autonomous campuses, new and different approaches to long range academic planning will be required. And if the university does not provide these innovations, there are others in the wings—in coordinating agencies and state capitals—eager to take over.

Some things remain the same—the gap between the ideal and the real, the autonomy of the individual professor, and the reluctance of state government to regard plans as more than prophecies. But much has changed, for organizations like individuals often show greater capacities in adversity. Reduced fiscal support, reduced enrollment, or both provide opportunity and demand for academic leadership. This is evident in the quantitative and qualitative improvement in the process and results of academic planning during the past five years. No longer merely responsive to external demands from state officials, multicampus systems have been forced by the imperatives of internal decision-making and resource allocation to develop planning capability at both the campus and the systemwide levels.

Planning and program review are not really separable; budgeting involves both. In our discussion we separate three activities that are becoming increasingly parallel and complementary. The difficulty of separate discussion suggests that the reported demise of program, planning, and budgeting systems (PPBS) may be premature. Just as M. Jourdain spoke prose without knowing it, many of the multicampus systems are combining the three activities of PPBS without the elaborate formal procedures, jargon, and emphasis on quantification associated with that term.

Nine Academic Plans

Formal plans of the nine multicampus systems under study range from highly general, sometimes cosmetic descriptions to carefully detailed, well-defined statements of goals and programs. Examination of these formal planning documents is necessary and useful, as suggested by the University of California (1975b, p. 6): "ongoing plans need to be crystallized and made explicit at appropriate intervals for a number of purposes: operating budget preparation, capital outlay planning, evaluation of scholarly directions and enrollment trends, coordination among academic units and among campuses, meeting reporting requirements . . . and the periodic encouragement of longer perspectives than those which tend to mark day-to-day developments."

Nevertheless, formal documents are less important than the planning process itself. Assessment of the progress which each system has made toward a rational planning process requires examination of planning organization, the environment in which planning takes place, and the history of each system. Six of the nine multicampus systems have formal planning documents; two others are preparing such documents; and only one neither has such a document nor proposes to issue one.

California State University and Colleges. The current formal planning document (California State University and Colleges, 1974a) is updated annually, it lists existing and proposed degree programs for each of 19 campuses over the next five years. The plan includes information on enrollment allocation by campus over the five-year period, and graphs portray the disciplinary emphasis of each campus in relation to the others in the system. Campus profiles indicate campus deviation from the system mean along such dimensions as age and source of students, enrollment distribution by level, and full-time student status. The plan discusses selective systemwide interests or concerns, such as a review of existing programs. The plan is operational in the sense that after governing board approval of degree programs proposed in the plan, the central administration is empowered (but not required) to approve specific proposals for implementation.

University of California. The current academic plan (University of California, 1974e) supercedes a similar 1969 plan; a five-year planning cycle replaces the prior ten-year cycle. The plan will become operational in conjunction with more specific campus statements being developed in 1975 together with additional analysis of problems and issues confronting the system as a whole. The plan inventories current degree offerings of the nine campuses, and contains brief campus profiles. Major emphasis is given to university goals and objectives in the context of declining growth of fiscal support and enrollment, the latter being projected over a ten-year period for each campus. Planning and review processes and special priorities and concerns for the five-year planning period are discussed.

University of Illinois. The current plan (University of Illinois, 1974) replaces a 1970 provisional development plan. The plan describes a planning framework of general system and specific campus missions. University procedures for review of new and existing programs are discussed. Specific academic programs cited in the plan are divided into four categories: existing programs, which are not inventoried; approved new programs requiring funding or coordinating agency approval; proposed programs currently under internal review; and anticipated programs not yet formally under review. Projected enrollments for the planning period are stable for the two general campuses, but show a planned growth for the medical center. Appendices discuss and project fiscal needs and state funding.

University of Missouri. The academic plan issued in 1974 (University of Missouri, 1974b), is limited to degree programs and replaces a plan issued in 1968. Subsequent plans in preparation in 1975 will cover research, extension, and administration. The plan briefly discusses universitywide responsibilities, the policies behind and purposes of the plan, the goals of the four campuses, and the assumptions guiding program decisions. The plan is a detailed categorization of all existing and proposed degree programs in categories ranging from programs that are primary candidates for development to those to be terminated. Specific programs are footnoted to indicate cooperative multicampus degrees and programs, primarily, but not entirely, in advanced graduate study. The plan is operational in that it states specific program decisions. Enrollment projections are not stated in the plan itself.

City University of New York. Both the City and State Universities of New York are required by statute to prepare master plans every four years and to prepare progress reports midway between plans. The state education department comments on the plans, which also require approval of the governor. Both systems are operating under master plans prepared in 1972, and each prepared progress reports in 1974.

   The 1972 Master Plan (City University of New York, 1972) states general system and campus missions. It specifically discusses population and other trends in New York City and experience with the open admissions policy. Academic programs are listed for the six senior colleges, the nine community colleges, and the graduate center, and are categorized as "presently offered," "being developed," and "under consideration." Enrollment projections in the 1972 plan showed growth through 1980, with decreasing increments toward the end of the period. *The 1974 Progress Report* comments on these projections (City University of New York, 1974d, p. v): "The period of rapid expansion in student enrollment has come to an end. The University is revising downward the enrollment projections made in 1972 and is now estimating an essentially steady enrollment (rather than modest enrollment increases) at least through the end of the decade. This revision is based primarily on the general decline in the student college-going rate, a phenomenon experienced by many institutions of postsecondary education throughout the country over the past several years."

State University of New York. The master plan of the State University (State University of New York, 1972b) is unique in being developed through a blue-ribbon citizens' commission staffed by faculty, students, and administrators, which "deliberated for almost two years." Recommendations range from general—"plans will be drawn for the development of universitywide doctoral programs in selected fields which will draw upon the resources of faculty and facilities across the entire system" (p. 33), to campus-specific—"the New York State College of Ceramics at Alfred University will alter or augment its undergraduate and graduate programs to reflect new changes in industry and technology" (p. 49). Enrollments for the system as a whole are projected to 1980-81, and separate undergraduate/ graduate ratios are established collectively and not by the individual campuses for the four university centers and the 14 university colleges.

The plan is not operational in the sense of ratifying specific degree programs, but neither is it a mere cataloging of the obvious. It is, in the words of the chancellor, "the beginning of discussion, not the end . . . an agenda for policy discussion and a springboard for action, rather than a set of directives."

University of North Carolina. Like the University of Wisconsin, the University of North Carolina is midstream in academic planning: substantial administrative effort continues to be required to unify previously independent systems and campuses into a single system, and a moratorium on new programs maintained the status quo while planning structures were being developed. The major planning effort following merger has been preparation of the state plan for desegregation, completed early in 1974 to comply with HEW guidelines. An inventory of existing academic programs of three doctoral-granting campuses and 13 four- and five-year campuses was also prepared. Campus plans are being prepared for incorporation into a 1975-1980 systemwide plan under the assumption that existing programs define the role and scope of each campus. The administrative memorandum initiating the planning process states that one of the purposes of planning is to "enable the university to respond to the special problems posed by . . . the limited prospective growth or (in some cases) the decline in enrollments" (University of North Carolina, 1974b).

University of Wisconsin. Following merger legislation in 1971, existing academic programs were inventoried and program aspirations were reviewed. Twenty-five open hearings were held throughout the state to develop a brief but relatively specific mission statement (University of Wisconsin, 1974b). Missions are stated for the system as a whole and for the two doctoral campuses, 11 four- and five-year campuses, 14 campuses in the two-year center system, and extension. During development of the mission statement, a systemwide review of existing master's-level programs was conducted. System planning task forces are reviewing specific program areas to determine universitywide goals and needs. Campuses are developing ten-year academic plans based on goals outlined in the mission statement which will be incorporated into a systemwide plan identifying specific programmatic intentions for 1975-80 and long range goals for the subsequent five-year period (see, however, comments concerning phase-out and phase-down plans below).

While the University of Texas has not developed academic plans on a systemwide basis, campus plans subject to system approval are required (see, for example, University of Texas, 1974c). The system coordinates campus plans to avoid unnecessary duplication, but there is no attempt to integrate campus statements into a formal universitywide document.

Characteristics of Planning

Political factors. The ability of a multicampus system to plan and implement plans depends on the degree to which society as a whole and governmental agencies encourage and respect such plans. Despite considerable rhetoric, such encouragement is often lacking. To be sure, there are examples of academic planning decisions—differentiation of function between the two systems of California, for example—which have stood the test of time. In contrast, two universities perceive planning to be fruitless, even unwise: the University of Texas because of state politics, and the City University of New York because of racial, ethnic, labor, and religious problems in the city as well as New York City politics. (The City University does issue a formal master plan every four years but, we suggest, only because of the statutory requirement to do so.)

It should not be inferred that substantial informal or ad hoc planning is not taking place in these two systems. In both, planning is evidenced by system persuasion, budget review, and universitywide cooperation. The consortium of the three University of Texas campuses in Dallas, for example, is a model of selective multicampus operation. The president of the University of Texas School of Nursing operates six schools throughout the state from the central offices of the system. Similarly, the innovative baccalaureate program of the City University of New York is centrally based at the graduate school and university center. The graduate school itself is a self-regulating unit for doctoral programs in the City University. But there are limits to what each institution can do by way of formal academic planning in its particular political environment.

No one in the City University central offices questions the educational policy decision to institute open admissions. All, however, are equally and continuously aware of the political pressures which required it, and of the enormous problems and costs of physical space and remedial education which dominate all academic policy decisions. City politics is pervasive: the mayor appoints the chairman of the governing board, the governor appoints the vice-chairman, and individual members represent political voting blocs, ethnic constituencies, and religious affiliations. Borough presidents negotiate with the university over campus programs. A particular neighborhood can bring pressure to change a community college into a four-year one, and then alter its mission from career preparation to liberal arts.

The University of Texas comprises six general campuses, but the establishment of these campuses was not the result of comprehensive planning. Specific ad hoc decisions shaped the institution over the past decade. For example, Arlington became part of the University of Texas in 1965 through legislative action initiated by faculty on the campus and with little or no university impact on the decision. In much the same way, the gift to the state of the privately supported Graduate Center of the Southwest was transformed into a senior-level campus in Dallas (15 minutes from Arlington) in 1969 The Permian Basin campus at Odessa was a gift of the Texas legislature. The new four-year campus in San Antonio is the only one planned by the system from its inception.

Neither the City University nor the University of Texas

can be criticized for lack of operational plans, for formal planning is impossible. To the extent circumstances allow, these institutions pursue systemwide objectives by encouraging and monitoring cooperation, diversity, and specialization among their campuses. But with little or no fault of their own, both may be ambushed by enrollment declines which they foresee but for which they cannot adequately prepare.

Racial issues. Since the mid-1960s, few academic plans fail to address equal educational opportunity through student distribution by race. Plans of multicampus systems concerning equal access do not differ from plans of a single campus, with two exceptions. While race does not dominate planning in either the University of North Carolina or the City University of New York, it is such a major factor that the difference between these two universities and others seems one of kind and not of degree. Issues in the two systems, however, are not the same.

The policy of offering every high school graduate in New York City the opportunity to enroll at some campus of the City University was implemented in the fall of 1970. The numbers of black and Spanish-surnamed students increased dramatically (City University of New York, 1974d, pp. 1-2): From fall 1969 to fall 1973, the number of black first-time freshmen increased from 2,774 to 10,221 and Spanish-surnamed from 15,987 to 22,419; the two groups combined increased from 20 percent of total first-time freshmen to 41 percent.

The City University *1972 Master Plan* states that the "foremost priority of the 1970s will continue to be to make open admissions a success, not only as an admissions policy, but also as an educational program" (1972, p. 5). By enlarging its pool of possible applicants, City University has delayed and may avoid enrollment decline. It also has created major physical capacity problems that require the university to rent a large share of its space. The 1972 plan also states that the "high degree of uncertainty engendered by open admissions and the gross lack of facilities preclude" making enrollment projections by campus (City University of New York, 1972, p. 69); absence of such projections clearly inhibits individual campus planning.

Although proposed programs are listed in the 1972 plan as "being developed" or "under consideration" on a campus-by-campus basis, in fact individual programs and campus missions are influenced by racial and ethnic groups with little reference to the formal plan. If the central offices did not exercise detailed and almost daily systemwide control through admissions procedures and program review, campuses would change in fairly predictable ways—Queens would become predominantly white with few remedial programs; City College would become predominantly black and perhaps lose its traditionally high quality graduate offerings. The City University, like the University of Texas, is inhibited in its academic planning by local and state politics. At the City University, partisan political considerations are compounded by those of race and ethnicity.

In the University of North Carolina, the issue of race is raised by federal enforcement of civil rights statutes. In its planning process and in the ultimate plan, the system—unlike the City University—is formally responsible to an external agency. For example, the memorandum calling for campus plans (University of North Carolina, 1974b) states that "commitments made to HEW in the desegregation plan will require that special attention be given to the possibility of racially significant program duplications among institutions, and a study must be made of the qualitative deficiencies of the predominantly black institutions and what additional financial investment and other actions will be necessary to eliminate any deficiencies found."

The substance of this special attention is detailed in correspondence clarifying the commitment to HEW in the long range academic planning process (University of North Carolina, 1974c):

> The Board of Governors committed itself to undertake as a part of its current (1974-75) long range planning program a special effort to identify and evaluate possible instances of racially-based duplication of programs as between predominantly black and predominantly white institutions. . . . The program duplication and role definition studies will give special

attention to the instances of possibly unnecessary
program duplication between proximate pairs of predominantly white and predominantly black institutions, and seek revision in program responsibilities
aimed at the elimination of racially-based alternative
program offerings in those institutions.

The University of North Carolina will be held accountable
for the implementation of the desegregation plan through semi-
annual reports to the civil rights division of HEW. Desegregation
may have more influence on the academic plan than systemwide
administrators themselves suspect. Accountability to the federal
government is a priority which cannot be ignored.

Specificity of program intentions. Procedural review of new and
existing academic programs is discussed in the following chapter, but the usual first hurdle for new programs is inclusion in
the systemwide academic plan. Even existing programs must
overcome this hurdle when planning begins anew, as in North
Carolina and Wisconsin.

Formal academic plans at best are two-dimensional snap-
shots of an ongoing multidimensional process. They only hint at
the complexity that sometimes requires a delay in the resolution of issues. Yet such plans portray the results of planning,
and they are usually all that the public sees. They require discussion and evaluation even at the risk of oversimplification. As
noted above, academic plans range from general to specific. The
statements of the Universities of California and Missouri are
illustrative.

Of the nine systems, only the Universities of California and
Missouri give major planning consideration to allocation of advanced graduate work among campuses. Their academic plans
meet this problem in quite contrasting ways.

The University of Missouri plan lists all existing and proposed programs of its four campuses in five categories: programs that are primary candidates for development, secondary
candidates for development, to be continued at present levels,
candidates for reduction, and to be terminated. The plan was

achieved only after protracted—sometimes acrimonious—discussion and negotiation. A costly review of all doctoral programs by outside evaluation teams was intended to ensure that difficult decisions of program allocation would be embodied in the academic plan. Some observers doubt that hard decisions have been made and suggest that cooperative systemwide doctoral programs proposed in the plan are really compromises to avoid such decisions as denying a particular doctoral program to a campus. Yet even critics concede that such cooperative programs may succeed. Proposed multicampus programs are specifically designed for the Missouri situation of relatively limited resources and four graduate campuses. Programmatic considerations aside, however, the probability of success must be weighed against the heavy costs in time, dollars, and—in some instances —good will that were paid to obtain specificity in the plan.

With a similar problem but a generally stronger research and advanced graduate base, the University of California 1974 draft academic plan was more general. Hard and specific decisions were made in severely cutting projected enrollments for several developing campuses, but with respect to academic programs, the plan specifically stated that it would be operational only in conjunction with campus plans to be submitted in 1975. Campus plans are to be developed within the broad policies stated in the system plan and more specific administrative guidelines and, like the university plan, will be public documents subject to governing board approval. The third major element in the planning process will be an annual campus planning statement, a largely quantitative and internal administrative document. This internal document together with campus plans "will serve the purposes of budgetary development . . . [and] be of great importance for program review" (University of California, 1974b).

Much is to be said for the proposed process, particularly in its integration of planning and budgeting. Campus plans and systemwide analysis of them will unquestionably provide greater specificity. It is anticipated that the annual campus planning statements will play a major role in program allocation and will eliminate the prolonged agony of making all such decisions at one time, as in the Missouri system. It is hoped that these added reports will overcome concerns expressed over the generality of the initial systemwide plan, a concern addressed in *Academic Plan, Phase II* (University of California, 1975b), presented to the governing board in March 1975.

The academic plans of the University of Illinois and the California State University and Colleges rank between the more specific and the more general. The Illinois plan details proposed programs in three categories: programs approved by the governing board but either unfunded by the state or not yet approved by the coordinating agency; programs undergoing internal review within the university; and programs which are contemplated, but not yet formally submitted for review. No great insight is required to see the last category as a convenient bin to hold difficult decisions until another day; in fact, however, contemplated programs are the subject of substantial negotiation between the central offices and each campus.

The annual plans of the California State University and Colleges propose degree programs according to projected dates of initiation over the next five years. Any one plan gives the appearance of high specificity comparable to that of the University of Missouri plan. Examination of plans over the years, however, belies this appearance. Programs are not necessarily implemented five years after they appear in an annual plan; instead, everything "to the right of the line" is subject to renegotiation every year. Changing student demands, campus emphases, enrollment trends, and numerous other factors enter into annual negotiations between central administration and campuses. In effect, then, each annual plan represents specific campus aspirations approved by the central administration but still subject to board approval. Although the central administration is more likely to approve a program to be implemented five years hence than one to be funded in the next annual budget, more distant programs, as in the University of Illinois, are by no means automatically included.

Will any of these planning processes prove more effective than others, as changing student numbers, quality, and demands force difficult program allocation decisions? There is little expe-

rience on which to base an answer, but at this early stage, the
middle ground occupied by the University of Illinois and the
California State University and Colleges appears most promising. Lack of specificity invites the criticism that issues are not
being faced and may lead to faculty suspicion that the annual
operational budgetary decisions are less concerned with qualitative factors than with fiscal ones. On the other hand, great specificity may entail heavy costs and may force unneeded or
unwise decisions or compromises.

Physical facilities. Existing physical facilities, the existing faculty complement, and ongoing academic programs are the start-
ing point for academic planning. The latter two multicampus
considerations are discussed in later chapters. Physical facilities
(and related capital planning) are not a specific object of this
inquiry, but have obvious implications for academic planning.
In brief, planning is set in concrete, and planners and decision-
makers must accept the costs with which previous planning (or
nonplanning) has endowed the institution.
      At the multicampus level, underutilized or highly special-
ized facilities take different forms. None of the nine systems
confront the imminent closure of a campus as, for example, has
been recommended in Montana, although the University of Wisconsin has established a planning framework for such a decision
(University of Wisconsin, 1975). In the University of Missouri,
the Rolla campus, with declining enrollment, a highly specialized mission, and a rural location, might be a prime candidate
for closure, but the $60 million plant is specialized for the cam-
pus mission, cannot be moved, and is of little use for any other
purpose in the region. The continuing ability of Rolla to place
its practically oriented graduate engineers is a valid educational
justification for its maintenance, but the primary reason for its
continued presence in the new university academic plan is simply that it is there.
      In the University of California system, the Riverside cam-
pus, smallest of eight general campuses, presents a somewhat
different problem—freshman applicants redirected to it from
UCLA, Berkeley, and other campuses at planned capacity fail to

show up. The state is reluctant to authorize additional facilities at the San Diego and Irvine campuses, where demand does exist, when 1,000 empty spaces remain unfilled at Riverside, but there is nothing the university can do to offset the smog-ridden image of the campus.

The impact of existing physical facilities on systemwide academic plans is less apparent elsewhere. In North Carolina, shortfalls in enrollment have occurred at particular campuses but it is unlikely that any physical plant overcapacity, present or anticipated, will seriously influence the developing academic plans. In fact, the five predominantly black campuses were created expressly to duplicate programs already in existence, and the underlying assumption of the state desegregation plan is that these five will continue as viable and separate institutions. Current planning must direct itself to continuing and improving these campuses, while simultaneously promoting desegregation at all campuses.

The State University of New York and the California State University and Colleges are similar to the University of North Carolina in this context. Their missions in undergraduate education are necessarily regional, and smaller institutions are part of the price. Individual campuses will assuredly experience enrollment difficulty, but in these systems, academic plans are not substantially influenced by physical plant capacity. The Universities of Illinois and Texas are also free of problems in this area. Chicago Circle presents the special planning problems of a central-city campus, more concerned with program emphasis than physical capacity. Although the University of Texas has campuses neither expected nor, we suspect, initially wanted, the loose and informal style of planning of this system can defer dealing with possible overbuilding at Permian Basin until a later day. A member of the Texas coordinating board persuasively warns that the state is on the verge of overbuilding in higher education, but his words appear lost amidst the 16 separate boards which govern the senior colleges and universities of that state.

In marked contrast, the City University of New York is in the unique position of being perceptibly underbuilt. Speaking of the expected leveling-off and possible decline in enrollments, one City University officer concedes that what looks like good planning is the result of two "accidents": open admissions which increased enrollment, and prior underfunding of capital outlay plans.

No such "accidents" confront Wisconsin, with its long history of numerous small campuses, occasionally underutilized classrooms and laboratories, and some unused dormitories (largely, it is reported, because legislative increases in nonresident tuition reduced enrollment from neighboring states). Here, the fiscal realities of enrollment declines are shaking the tradition of carrying the university mission to every corner of the state. In January 1975, the governor asserted that "the university system and the state should be planning *now* to reduce the scope and/or number of its array of higher educational institutions and programs . . . [to] carefully weigh the alternatives and make specific recommendations for phasing out, phasing down, or consolidating centers, campuses, colleges, and programs." The governor requested a plan by April 15, 1975, "including a statement of language to be inserted in the 1975-77 biennial budget which would authorize implementation of the plan" (State of Wisconsin, 1975). With facilities as with faculty, Wisconsin is among the first of the systems to have to bite the bullet of retrenchment. The *President's Report* (University of Wisconsin, 1975) provides ample and constructive evidence about the extent to which the multicampus university is—as we hypothesize—an effective organizational strategy to confront the unsteady state.

3

Academic Program Review

As students and dollars become scarce the review of proposed and existing programs becomes a critical element of multicampus governance. With limited resources, each new academic program can be added only at the expense of an existing activity. Central administration must require campuses to reassess priorities, and must review the results from a systemwide perspective. Academic specialization, diversity, and cooperation are explicit considerations in effective review of both existing and proposed programs. But such review does not come easily or cheaply and, indeed, requires educational statesmanship of the highest order. Have current trends been responsible for new types of systemwide activity, and for new ways of looking at the overall academic program of the institution?

Five years ago, review of new and existing academic programs was set in the midst of expanding campuses with increasing numbers of students and faculty. The following comments, written at that time, illuminate the environment of the period (Lee and Bowen, 1971, pp. 233-234):

> Academic program review has two distinct but interrelated aspects. The first concerns the *appropriateness* of a specific program proposal within the mission of the campus; this mission is sometimes expressed in a

formal academic plan but often found in a more general and informal understanding of campus goals . . . . The second element of program review involves the *readiness* of the campus to mount a program in terms of such matters as numbers and quality of faculty, library, and laboratory resources. The system serves as an internal accrediting agency. . . .

The useful role of the system in program review is most evident in the nurture of new campuses and, secondly, in the change in role and orientation accompanying the transition of an existing two- or four-year college into a university campus.

What is noteworthy in these comments is not what they say but what they omit. The emphasis in 1971 was on new and transitional campuses. Quality control rather than allocation of scarce resources marked the discussion, and concern over duplication focused largely on highly specialized doctoral programs. No more than passing reference is made to review of existing programs. While systemwide review of academic programs occasionally concerned itself with intercampus specialization and eliminating unnecessary duplication—the first act of the new University of North Carolina system in 1931 was to reallocate programs between Raleigh and Chapel Hill—the environment in which academic program review is now conducted is sharply different from that of five years ago.

Today, the implications for program review of stabilization or decline in enrollment and fiscal stringency are direct and explicit. Systemwide review of new academic programs has become more intensive, based on academic quality and campus mission in six or more of the nine systems and on fiscal criteria in eight. The change in existing program review procedures is more dramatic: Seven of the nine systems have instituted procedures for periodic review of existing graduate and professional programs. The current situation is well expressed in a discussion of review of new graduate programs in a 1974 academic plan (University of California, 1974e, pp. 18-19): "During the period of rapid university growth in the 1960s . . . the approval of new

graduate programs in the university depended almost exclusive-
ly upon favorable academic review. The new conditions of
slower growth and the associated limitation of resources made
apparent the need for closer administrative scrutiny to assure
that resources for new programs would be allocated on the basis
of both approved campus and universitywide priorities."

By hindsight, it is easy to criticize earlier assumptions that
if a campus was competent to institute a new program it should
do so, and that any program in existence should continue without review. We shared the assumptions, however, to the extent
that we did not even ask about review of existing programs in
our earlier study. And, realistically, little else could have been
done. In the early part of the 1960s, the nine systems were fully
preoccupied with expansion to accommodate a seemingly endless number of applicants. In the latter part, student disorder
distracted university leadership from academic to custodial
responsibilities. It is to the credit of the nine systems that orderly processes of reviewing new programs were maintained
throughout the period and that, by and large, program quality
was not diluted through numbers of students.

It is unfortunate, however, that systematic review of existing programs and greater emphasis on fiscal criteria were not initiated at an earlier date. Procedures for reaching ultimate qualitative judgments are suspect if they appear to be undertaken for
purely fiscal reasons, particularly if the governing board orders
such review for the express purpose of terminating programs, as
occurred in the California State University and Colleges in
1971, during a budgetary crunch. Similarly, a systemwide
review was initiated by legislative mandate in Wisconsin, and
the objectivity of central administration in implementing review
was suspect. When the University of California linked program
review with annual budget cycles, some faculty objected that
academic decisions were being made by budget administrators
for budgetary reasons; acceptance is currently being sought by
involving faculty and campus administrators in critical aspects
of the review process.

Current academic plans generally discuss both existing and
proposed programs. As plans are implemented, procedures for

preparing specific new program proposals usually require campus or central administrative review of similar existing programs on other campuses. Conversely, planned or routine review of existing programs may require a closer scrutiny or deferral of new program proposals. Implicitly or explicitly, the stringency of procedures depends on the fiscal impact of a program. Increasingly, quantitative cost data are considered in the review process and are integrated with the university budget cycle.

The extent to which plans and program review are related in each of the nine systems, however, is influenced by the history of the system, the size, number, and age of its campuses, the political climate, and any number of other variables, including the idiosyncrasies of administrators. Academic plans, usually printed, bound, and issued at a specific time for a public audience, are tangible and convey at least an illusion of solidity which permits classification. Program review procedures, however, are generally mimeographed, are not usually intended for an audience outside the institution (or interested state agencies on occasion), and vary across time and sometimes with the specific program being reviewed. Generalizations assuredly can be made, but classification is both difficult and hazardous.

New Programs

With individual variations, new program review procedures generally follow the pattern in Figure 1, adapted from a flow chart in the University of Illinois (1974) academic plan. Since 1970, changes in this pattern have been largely in two areas: a cleaning up of procedural loose ends and an overall increase in the intensity of review.

Increased intensity of new program review in eight of the nine systems is clearly attributable to fiscal stringency, declining enrollment growth, or both. The most objective evidence is found in moratoria on new program proposals, ranging from the broadest and longest in Wisconsin, which covered both graduate and undergraduate programs and lasted for three years, to a two-year moratorium in North Carolina, to restrictions in certain program areas in both California systems. In New York, approval of new doctoral programs in both systems was halted

Figure 1. Approval required for development of new programs

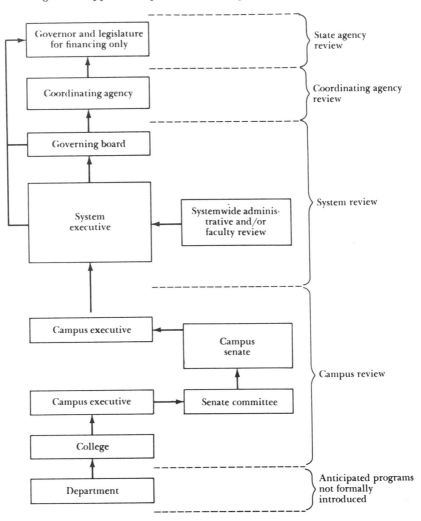

while the Fleming Commission prepared its report. At the other extreme is the simple policy statement by the State University of New York that systemwide offices would be more careful in reviewing new programs. Although it is not clear that the small staff could actually intensify review efforts, fewer programs were in fact sent up from the campuses.

From the viewpoint of multicampus operations, fiscal stringency is reflected in the way that costs determine the form and extent of program review. For example, in North Carolina recently established program review procedures are initiated by a campus planning authorization request, which includes projections of faculty and other resources and potential student demand. A more detailed proposal is not necessary if "the program . . . does not include *new faculty positions or resources beyond presently approved support levels,* and provided further that it falls under one of the following categories: (1) a new arrangement of existing courses, (2) new options within previously authorized degree programs, (3) a degree offering lower than an already approved offering in the same academic field" (University of North Carolina, 1974a).

Categorization by cost in the Universities of North Carolina and California makes fiscal concerns explicit. What appears unique in the University of California is the requirement that for new programs which entail substantial additional costs, the campus must present "convincing evidence that the objectives of the program cannot be effectively achieved by the establishment of a joint program with another campus (or campuses) of the university, with an associated saving in resources required" (University of California, 1972).

In every system, new program proposals must project future resources required, usually for five years. But the integration of cost projections with operating budgetary procedures is far from complete. Attempts to mesh program review and budgeting are underway at the Universities of Wisconsin and California, but these are the exception (and even in these two institutions, actual integration of review and budgeting is not expected until procedures have been tested through several budget cycles).

Traditional administrative separation of academic planning and budgeting can prove a barrier to integration. For example, in North Carolina differences must be resolved between campus enrollment figures furnished to the system for budgetary purposes and those furnished to the planning office. A somewhat more subtle problem is found in the California State University and Colleges. The major component of State University budgets is detailed determination of faculty staffing levels by the academic affairs office, which plays a major role in budgetary decisions both internally and in contacts with state agencies. During program review, however, review of costs other than those for faculty is not fully integrated with the university budget office.

The most detailed attempt to determine cost implications of new programs has been made at the University of Missouri. Anticipating consideration of a new systemwide academic plan, the governing board asked that it be costed out by central administration. In general, the products of the National Center for Higher Education Management Systems (NCHEMS) were used to determine average cost per student based on 1973 expenditures. Procedures assumed that dollars would remain constant through 1979-80, and that the only additional resources would be directly related to projected enrollment increases. Campuses were then asked to allocate projected total dollars among academic programs in accordance with the academic plan's five-way categorization of new and existing programs (primary or secondary candidates for development, and to be continued, reduced, or terminated). It was presumed that where programs were to be improved according to the academic plan, costs per student would increase, balanced by either increased productivity or fewer students in less favored programs. Briefly, departments were required to shuffle finite numbers of students and dollars to reflect stated program priorities. Despite a restricted time frame, the exercise required departmental faculty as well as campus administrators to address the operational implications of resource reallocation, meeting a common complaint that, in many institutions, "grass-roots faculty" are not yet fully aware of the implications of declining enrollment growth.

Although financial ability to mount a program is an important aspect of program review, program appropriateness and campus readiness continue to be major factors. Indeed, concerns over the appropriateness of specific programs have increased. It is no longer true that campus missions are more often found in an informal understanding of campus goals than in formal academic plans. In the past five years, most of the nine multicampus systems have developed reasonably specific academic plans and, either as a part of or in conjunction with such plans, have instituted review procedures which emphasize separation of program appropriateness from campus readiness to undertake it.

Campuses tend to hope that enrollment difficulties will end if a new program is approved. Fortunately, there is no indication that campuses are proposing—or systemwide offices approving—programs of less than traditional quality to attract more students. The use of program evaluators from outside the university, selected by system offices, as is required at the University of Texas for all new graduate degree programs, provides an additional guarantee of campus readiness.

Inclusion in the academic plan is a first hurdle for academic programs in most systems. In Missouri, new programs appear in the academic plan either as primary or secondary candidates for development. (Of ten proposed new Ph.D. programs in the current plan, six are indicated as being cooperative programs among two or more campuses.) The task of reviewing proposed new programs for their appropriateness was part of the three-year development of the academic plan itself. This difficult, costly, and time-consuming task entailed outside review of all academic programs at all campuses. Exact procedures for the second step of review—the readiness of a campus to undertake a program—were issued in late 1974. The first step may have been unnecessarily all-inclusive and drawn out. As a wise system executive said in another context, "With limited resources, it is best not to give everything and take everything at the same time." However, the University of Missouri was faced with an immediate political and resource problem of allocating doctoral programs among very different campuses. The difficulty of the problem may justify the exception to the more incremental approach found in such systems as University of Illinois and California State University and Colleges.

In Illinois, proposed new programs are listed simply as being under internal review or as anticipated but not formally introduced. In the California State University and Colleges, new programs are projected over the five years following annual revision of the systemwide planning document. Not every campus aspiration is placed on this time scale, nor, as previously noted do programs automatically advance from one year to the next; for example, a previously approved engineering technology program was disallowed because a similar one had been authorized 15 miles away at another California State University campus and enrollments did not justify further expansion. In more sophisticated ways, the extensive data system of the State University combines with the annual planning review to bring current systemwide experience to bear on questions of appropriateness of specific programs for specific campuses. Several campuses, for example, had projected master's programs in Spanish. A routine review of similar programs at nine other campuses enabled the system to give campuses with projected programs detailed information on enrollment, faculty, student credit hours, class size, and degree trends, and to provide indications of system approval: "Graduate Spanish has been identified in the attached systemwide performance review report as a low enrollment program on a number of campuses. Data for the undergraduate program indicate that _____ does not currently have the undergraduate base to support a quantitatively viable master's degree program. Undergraduate degree production has in fact declined continuously since 1966-67. The [central] office will therefore no longer be able to support projection of the MA in Spanish on the Academic Master Plan for _____ ."

In other systems, the initial decision on program appropriateness is determined outside the formal planning process. In the State University of New York, campuses file a letter of intent with the central administration to offer a new program. The denial of a campus proposal was accompanied by this statement: "While this will undoubtedly cause frustration among certain of your faculty and student body, the resources of the university, and in our judgment the resources of the college, are not adequate to initiate and sustain a major program in dance. The college at _____ as you know has invested heavily in a dance program and has a well-established reputation in your area of the state against which your nascent program would have to compete . . . . It is not possible to justify an additional B.A. program in the dance within the State University for the foreseeable future."

In the City University of New York system, a comparable procedure takes the form of early warning letters. Traditionally required only of community colleges, use of such letters is now being extended to four-year campuses. It should be noted that central administration of City University, unlike that of the other eight systems, lacks specific formal authority over academic programs. Program proposals originate at the campuses and are prepared by central administration for review by the governing board. With only ministerial authority, City University central administration must rely on its power of persuasion (which, however, is rarely overridden).

In the North Carolina system, a request for authorization to plan likewise allows early system review of the appropriateness of a program, as an internal staff memorandum makes clear: "*M.A. in Art Education*: [The campus] now offers no work in art or art education on the graduate level and proposes the addition of two additional faculty members by 1976-77. They project 25 students by that time. This projection, in view of the attendance and degree production history at [three other system campuses] is unrealistic. . . . The program would be duplicative in terms of projected needs . . . a recommendation that planning not be authorized seems appropriate."

Whether through the academic planning process directly or collaterally, early warning of proposals for new academic programs is very much a part of the administration of academic affairs in most of the nine multicampus systems. Such procedures recognize that the effort of preparing a full-scale proposal in 1975 is unequally balanced against the probability that it will be turned down.

Existing Programs

In the past five years, seven of the nine multicampus universities have initiated systemwide procedures for the periodic review of existing graduate and professional academic programs.[1] Five have initiated similar procedures for undergraduate programs. The importance of such review in an era of declining resources is explicit in planning documents. In the University of Wisconsin, a draft memorandum states (University of Wisconsin, 1974d):

> It is the Regent's policy that future program development in the system will rely heavily on base budget reallocation and/or resource redeployment at the institutional level; and that, therefore, *new program* intentions and proposals which become part of the system's long range academic plan will be closely linked with and often be dependent on the *existing program* reviews and intentions of the relevant institutions. In addition, it is important that in the context of existing program review each Institution identify and plan toward the modification, elimination, or consolidation of low demand, inefficient, and/or unnecessarily duplicative programs in general with an eye to reallocating and/or redeploying resources to the support of higher priority programs.

The president of a State University of New York campus sounds similar warnings (State University of New York, 1974a): "I have repeatedly indicated that—painful as this may be in cer-

---

[1] The Regents of the University of the State of New York (New York State Education Department, 1973) have initiated a "systematic evaluation and rating by the Commissioner of Education of all doctoral programs [public and private] in the state in each major subject area for the purpose of maintaining programs that meet standards of high quality and clear need, and improving or phasing out those not meeting high standards." Two such reviews (history and chemistry) were completed in 1974. "The evaluations have sparked a controversy over state control of academic programs, and have led to debate over the method to be used in any review of graduate education" ("Statewide Planning vs. University Autonomy," 1975). These statewide review procedures are omitted from this discussion of systemwide activity. Although highly relevant, they are beyond the scope of this study.

tain instances—we must set some clear priorities if we are to develop a reasonable number of genuinely strong graduate programs. . . . The current state of our programmatic development and the budget realities within which we must work in the 1970s simply make it impossible for us to think in terms of developing all of our graduate programs at the same level of emphasis."

Systemwide planners at California State University and Colleges state with candor: "Sometimes it's necessary to hold approval of a new program as ransom for elimination of an old one." This obvious relationship between new and existing programs is present at all higher education institutions when resources are scarce. In review of existing programs, however, administrators at multicampus systems are bound by considerations foreign to a single institution. One general goal is the elimination of unnecessary duplication or undue specialization in program offerings across campuses. On the other hand, as statewide systems, the Universities of North Carolina and Wisconsin have a clear obligation to serve all regions of their states, and duplication among regions is sometimes necessary. In addition, North Carolina is faced with historic and deliberate program duplication at predominantly black campuses. And where campuses have the mission of advanced graduate work, small and expensive programs may be unique to the state or even to the nation.

The obligation to preserve specialized programs cuts across all fields. Personnel difficulties, for example, are engendered by tenured faculty in the humanities, where enrollment declines are most evident. A senior university administrator not known for rhetoric recognizes the immediate fiscal problems in sustaining high cost humanities programs, but suggests that the major long term educational issue is the obligation of a major university to "preserve civilization."

Unlike systemwide review of new academic programs, procedures for review of existing programs do not fit any general pattern. They are discussed here as system-based and campus-based, but these categories are not mutually exclusive. System-based review requires varying degrees of campus involvement, and campus-based review is usually influenced by systemwide encouragement or direction.

Campus-based review. Generally, multicampus systems encourage or require campuses to review all graduate programs on a five-year cycle, or their campuses have independently developed procedures using such a cycle. The University of Wisconsin considers the campus-based procedures devised by the graduate faculty council at Milwaukee to be exemplary. Under the Milwaukee procedures, review is undertaken by an ad hoc committee of at least two voting members from the Milwaukee graduate faculty, one in a discipline related to the program under review and the others from an unrelated discipline. A third (and usually a fourth) voting member is an outside expert appointed by the dean of the graduate school from a list of nominees supplied by the council of graduate schools. The dean of the appropriate department is an ex officio member. Procedures set out a detailed format for information required of the department at the time that a review is undertaken.

While systemwide interest is not expressly stated in the documents themselves, it is implicit in the required approval of procedures by the central administration and governing board. The university system will continue the practice of approving doctoral programs at Milwaukee only if these are relevant to the urban thrust of that campus and not duplicative of Madison offerings. This specialized and noncompetitive mission is accepted despite at least one recent skirmish resulting in system disapproval of a proposed doctoral program in history.

The extent to which multicampus central administrations encourage or monitor campus-based program review varies substantially. In the Universities of Texas and California, for example, there has been no systemwide initiation or requirement of campus-based review, although campuses in both systems have undertaken such activity on their own.

In contrast, the University of Illinois has taken the positive position of requiring each of its three campuses to develop review procedures for existing programs, and administrators are particularly pleased with the response of the Urbana campus

(University of Illinois, 1974, p. 20): "The report of the Urbana-Champaign Study Committee on Program Evaluation (SCOPE) was recommended by the former Chairman of the Illinois Board of Higher Education to every institution of higher education in the State." Although so recommended, Urbana procedures are not followed by the other two campuses of the university. The Medical Center in Chicago coordinates internal program review of its highly specialized units with outside accreditation visits. Chicago Circle campus, perhaps understandably unwilling to adopt the procedures of its older and more prestigious sibling, is still searching for appropriate alternatives.

In the State University of New York, a similar system role is found in administrative approval of campus-based program review guidelines. The central staff describes their efforts as an attempt to "institutionalize campus activities that have often been desultory in the past." Central administration requires that periodic evaluation of existing graduate programs be made every five years and sets forth an outline of points to be covered in both the conduct of internal evaluation and in the report of an external evaluation team. Internal and external evaluation reports, the faculty unit response to the report, and comments of the campus graduate council, dean, and chief campus executive are submitted to central administration for review. The cognizant system officer is required to respond within 60 days indicating "approval of a program for a period, conditional approval for a limited time (in some instances involving a subsequent reevaluation), or nonapproval" (State University of New York, 1972a). A parallel campus-based evaluation effort is now being mounted under system leadership for undergraduate programs.

Like the State University of New York, the California State University and Colleges require campus program review procedures and review of these by systemwide staff. Again, a five-year cycle is required, but outside review, although used by some campuses, is not. University administrators encourage campuses to consider approved procedures of other campuses, but without any requirement that they be adopted. Major concerns of university administrators are the lack of common assessment criteria across campuses and the difficulties of central review of the mass of information furnished annually by 19 campuses. Results of campus-based reviews are annually summarized and reported to the governing board. For example (California State University and Colleges, 1973c): "California State University, Humboldt: A special committee approved the statement of goals and objectives of the institution which are to be used in program review. These are being translated into the criteria for formal program review in 1973-74. Consolidations in the areas of business and economics are being discussed, as well as consolidation of graduate natural resources programs."

Program review at the City University of New York is campus-based. Although uniform procedures are centrally established and systemwide interest in results is substantial, reviews are conducted of entire campuses, of specific master's programs, and of doctoral programs at the graduate center rather than of similar programs across campuses.[2]

None of these reviews, however, is responsive to real or anticipated declines in either enrollment or fiscal support. Campus evaluations grew out of governing board concern that academic quality be maintained as campuses adjusted to large numbers of previously unqualified students. Review of master's programs was initiated because of the concern of the New York State Regents about the unevenness in the quality of master's degree programs throughout the state. The primary purpose of each type of review is the improvement of individual campus program offerings.

Campus-based reviews in City University are based on self-studies and outside evaluation. Notification of proposed evaluation is given approximately nine months in advance. The campus prepares a self-study in accordance with a standard outline. The campus nominates at least six evaluators from outside City

[2]A fourth form of review, not discussed here, is of campus implementation of the City University open-admissions policy. The systemwide effort at assessment is commendable, and would justify inquiry by those contemplating similar evaluations, for example, of affirmative action. Neither the unique open-admissions procedure nor more general affirmative action policies are within the purview of the present study.

University, one each from the physical sciences, the social sciences, the humanities, student affairs, libraries, and administration. It may nominate others based on the curricular thrust of the campus. The City University chief executive can make additional appointments. The evaluation team receives the self-study a month before it visits the campus for four days. The team report of findings and recommendations on issues set out in review procedures is sent simultaneously to the campus and system chief executives. After review by these executives, the governing board considers the recommendations with them in executive session. Review of master's programs follows a substantially similar procedure.

Although oriented to a single campus, these procedures have implications for City University as a multicampus institution, and central administrators actively monitor both the self-study and the evaluation team activities. Indeed, one of the five objectives assigned to the evaluation teams is to identify programs that can be shared with other campuses in the system.

A parallel procedure is followed by City University in review of doctoral programs, each of which is slated for evaluation every five years. It is likely, however, that such reviews will not prove influential in resource allocation decisions confronting the graduate center or central administration. While external political factors may play less of a role at the doctoral than the undergraduate level, the facts of City University life, and the continuing contest between the graduate center and the campuses, will prove more influential than formal program review.

System-based review. In general, review of existing academic programs at the system level takes place only when a specific need arises. Such reviews are not necessarily one-time exercises, however; procedures developed for one purpose often continue for others. Categorization is difficult, but most system-based review procedures can be classified either as selective or comprehensive. Selective reviews are of more narrow program areas over time; comprehensive reviews are of all degree programs over a shorter time frame.

Three multicampus systems offer examples of selective,

system-based review of existing programs: the Universities of California and Wisconsin and California State University and Colleges. Review procedures are considered an integral part of the planning process, and all are relatively new.

In the University of California, the academic planning and program review board (APPRB) is responsible for review of new program proposals and budget recommendations. In addition, it reviews existing program offerings through ad hoc committees of faculty representatives and others from outside the university. The function of the board in reviewing existing programs is described in the academic plan (University of California, 1974e, p. 20):

> The board may select for review any subject area whose development appears to have significant implications for the achievement of the university's planning objectives. Disciplinary areas marked for early attention are those in which proposals have been made for introduction or expansion of work on a number of campuses, or in which substantial changes in student demand or social need suggest the desirability of reevaluation of total offerings and associated activities. . . . The criteria used in cross-campus reviews will be similar to those used in the review of new program proposals, but they will, of course, be applied simultaneously to all the individual programs in a specific disciplinary area across the campuses."

One such review committee was asked to evaluate existing programs in a given field at several campuses and to comment on a proposed program at a particular campus. In its final recommendations, the committee concluded that "it would hinder the entire . . . system to add another small, struggling school . . . at a time when existing programs are in need of additional qualified students."[3]

---

[3] Review committee recommendations were not limited to specific campuses. Committee comment on the need for systemwide coordination is

After receiving the report, the systemwide review board, through the system chief executive, referred it to campuses for comment. The campus chief executive and the faculty senate were asked three specific questions concerning possible effects of upgrading, limiting, or terminating the program: "(1) If the central review board should recommend upgrading the program, what resources would be needed, and how would they be made available? (2) If there were no recommendation to upgrade the program, how could the scope of the program be limited to improve its quality? (3) If the decision were made to terminate the program, what impact would such termination have on other campus programs and activity?" Systemwide administrators stress both quality of review and importance of careful implementation of review recommendations. Campus administrators and faculty are advised of all options open to them and to the system, and campuses are offered an opportunity for response.

At the University of Wisconsin, system planning task forces are undertaking more general but similar assignments. These review groups are directly concerned with development of the systemwide academic plan and are considered a primary vehicle for development of specific statewide programmatic objectives. Nine task forces cover disciplines such as business administration, health sciences, and engineering, and overarching systemwide concerns such as women's studies and computers.

The charge of the systemwide administration to the system planning task force on business administration is typical (University of Wisconsin, 1973c):

---

particularly noteworthy since it comes from a committee composed largely of faculty, albeit one appointed by central administration: "We concluded that the individual campuses are largely unaware of what is happening in [similar programs] on the other campuses and we suspect that, up to this point, no one at statewide has been accurately informed, either. Regardless of the degree of formal planning and control that might be exercised from a systemwide point of view, we suggest that [the systemwide administration] designate some individual or committee to monitor the progress and development of the various schools and programs on a continuing basis in the future."

The major purpose of the task force will be the development of recommendations for a system long range plan for business administration. These recommendations which are based upon an inventory of current program offerings need to concern the following: (a) system goals for programing in the functional fields of business administration; (b) adequacy of existing programs to meet current or anticipated societal needs; (c) identification of existing programs which should be changed or developed in relationship to current or projected societal needs; (d) need for additional programs in business administration, including the particular criteria by which proposals for such programs should be examined and considerations which would be pertinent to any new program approvals.

The use of as many as nine task forces for program review is a special and doubtless one-time attempt to obtain in-depth advice and comment from a broad spectrum. The continued use of special task forces in a more limited fashion is anticipated after the academic plan is adopted. These are described as special audits or lateral reviews, to be initiated when a new program proposal appears to duplicate offerings across campuses. Final procedures for this activity are under development.

Selective system-based review at California State University and Colleges differs substantially from that at the Universities of California and Wisconsin. Utilizing an extensive data base, systemwide academic administrators identify specific problems of quantitative concern on individual campuses and request campus review of these. For example, campus review of a master's program in economics was initiated when cross-campus quantitative data indicated that degree production was substantially lower than that in comparable programs elsewhere in the system. Substantive review indicated that low degree production was in part attributable to probationary admission of students, a procedure considered an essential part of the program at the urban commuter campus. In addition, however, students were transferring from the campus to nearby institutions to complete their degrees because of unreasonable course requirements. System administrators emphasize that their role is to call attention to apparent program difficulties, not to make decisions based on the quantitative data. Qualitative program decisions are considered to be the province of the campuses.

Two examples of comprehensive system-based review of existing academic programs indicate both the difficulty and the far-reaching implications such review may have. (A third example, a review of master's programs at each of the ten colleges of arts and science of the State University of New York was initiated in the fall of 1974.) By far the broadest review was conducted by the University of Missouri, primarily during 1972 and 1973, but continuing into 1974. During this period, 30 external evaluation teams spent a week in Missouri surveying both graduate and undergraduate programs. Each team generally had four members, carefully selected for both academic achievement and administrative experience; none had been educated or employed in the University of Missouri. Teams were formed around either a broad discipline, such as biological sciences, a group of related disciplines, such as agriculture, home economics, and forestry, or functional areas such as research or computers. Systemwide administration collected and furnished to teams objective and subjective information from departments to be evaluated.

The charge to teams varied, according to the perceptions of systemwide administrators of the major problems requiring evaluation in each subject area. In general, teams were requested to enumerate program strengths and weaknesses, to give recommendations of support or termination of the program, and to suggest new program phases to be established (see University of Missouri, 1973a).

Written reports were submitted four weeks after campus visits and were utilized in development of the new academic plan. Some reports touched on the multicampus aspect of programs, noting the need for particular concentrations at particular campuses, as well as the utilization of systemwide facilities, such as the computer network and the reactor laboratory. In general, system administrators state that reports candidly answered questions posed, and this information was supplemented by discussions between the team and the system chief executive which concluded each visit. The evaluation effort has been criticized by some as shallow, and because of the breadth of objectives and the limited time, the criticism would appear to have some justification. On the other hand, the systemwide administration, concerned though it might be with programs at particular campuses, was under pressure to obtain an overall evaluation of programs across all campuses within a very short period of time. Evaluation teams had more extensive information about departments, degree programs, and faculty than is often routinely available at the systemwide level. Moreover, evaluation team members constituted a highly select group of nationally known and widely experienced professionals.

Systemwide administration in Missouri is pleased with the specific contribution which the evaluations made to the development of the academic plan. Perhaps more important, they are convinced that both campus faculty and administrators now recognize that there is a multicampus potential for development of disciplines. While this conviction might more properly be classed as a hope, university administrators express confidence that this recognition will undergird the structural programmatic changes that are envisaged in cooperative systemwide doctoral programs now being established.

In the University of Missouri, overall review was required by the urgent need for explicit statement of program priorities. In the University of Wisconsin, however, an overall review was undertaken in response to pressure from the legislature. The review was broad, covering all master's programs in the system. The first step in the review process was entirely at the systemwide level, where quantitative data—enrollments, class size, degree output, and the like—were used to classify all master's programs into those which should be continued, those which it seemed appropriate to terminate, and those which should be subject to further review in two years. Campus faculty and administrators then reviewed the classification, and differences between campus and central administration recommendations were discussed, with central administration generally accepting campus views.

In the final report (University of Wisconsin, 1974e) the first recommendation—phase-out of 51 programs—is the most striking, but probably the least important. Described by a system administrator as "cats and dogs," elimination of these programs will result in minimal cost savings. The second and third recommendations—actual and possible program consolidation—pertain to internal campus matters. The fourth recommendation —marking 60 programs for two-year review—is also an internal campus matter, but one which requires comment in the multicampus context.

Conventional wisdom holds that centralization of authority is the inevitable result of hard times and hard decisions. A view of the entire program review process, however, and particularly the two-year review recommendation, indicates that in the University of Wisconsin at least, the need for difficult decisions has resulted in decentralization. Central administration does not enforce program decisions in the budgetary process. Rather, the policy is to confront campuses with questions raised by quantitative and comparative data, and force decisions at the operational level. Reported response from campuses reflects the tensions that are inherent in every multicampus system, although some are specific to the newly merged University of Wisconsin. At least some campus administrators and perhaps some faculty would rather not have to make decisions which appear required: it is easier to accept a program cut handed down from the central offices than to impose one on friends and colleagues.

The fifth Wisconsin recommendation—system or regional review for 78 programs—will be discussed in Chapter Five. It is of interest here, however, for regional coordination emerged as an unintended consequence of this program review. The reviews here reported—for new and existing programs, system- or campus-based, comprehensive or selective—are the forerunners of the critical resource and program analyses which will increasingly undergird academic decision-making in the 1980s.

4

Academic Budgeting

If changing enrollments are the principal cause of the unsteady state, budgets are the principal effect. Cost has always been a consideration in academic program decisions, but fiscal factors now loom even larger. Identification of true costs (and benefits) on a systemwide basis and implementation of decisions based on cost identifications have become essential. The implications of constant funding (often actually reduced by inflation) are found in virtually every aspect of academic administration. Budgetary procedures developed while enrollment was growing rapidly may not be applicable as enrollments stabilize; states often attempt to achieve economies at the cost of system flexibility, at the same time that increased internal reallocations are necessary. How can flexibility be retained as constant dollars are eroded by inflation? Is systemwide flexibility achieved only by reducing the flexibility of campuses?

Five years ago we quoted the words of one system executive that "the operating budget is the single most important educational document in the university." We went on to say: "Here, the academic goals of faculty, administrators, and students confront the societal values of governors, legislators, and taxpayers. In the budgetary process, academic governance receives its most severe challenge" (Lee and Bowen, 1971, p. 247). Today the budget is, if possible, even more important.

Enrollment stabilization and inflation have increased the visibility of budgetary decisions; there are more participants in the process. Multicampus systems are under greater pressure—from both the campuses and the capital—to demonstrate that they are effective administrators of scarce resources. While the basic outlines of university·budgeting remain much the same, central administrations are developing new and more effective quantitative measures for resource allocation and appropriate cross-campus comparisons. Budgeting is more sophisticated. However, while the need for flexibility in budget administration in times of scarcity has generally been recognized by state budget officers, state fiscal requirements still dominate the process. These can prove insensitive to the problems of multicampus systems in an unsteady state.

The major change in the past five years, however, is not in technical budgetary procedures but in a closer relationship between budgeting and academic planning. In the past, as one systemwide budget officer stated, "the planning people were always off somewhere in the future; now they're being as hard nosed about costs as we are—maybe harder." A working paper in the State University of New York (1973, p. V-7) discusses the distance between program planning and budgeting during the years of extremely rapid growth: "Academic planning in the early and mid-1960s reflected both state educational needs, which seemed almost limitless, and institutional ambitions. Campuses and programs were initiated and began to flourish. Hundreds of thousands of students were enrolled and graduated. Necessary funds were almost always available to develop and expand programs, and academic planning seemed not to have to be unduly concerned with financial consequences. Perhaps a statewide university of such great promise could not have been created any other way."

Three related issues are of importance: the impact of various enrollment computations and their use in the budgetary process; fiscal flexibility and its uses in the multicampus context; and state intervention into university academic matters through budgetary procedures. Technical budgetary procedures can set boundaries to flexibility, as can more substantive state governmental interest in accountability for the use of funds. All have substantial impact on academic plans and program review.

Enrollment

Numbers of students and numbers of dollars are brought into balance at the nine multicampus systems through widely differing formulas and guidelines. Details of these procedures are complex and go beyond the purview of this study. Two issues are of interest, however, because of their relevance to current uncertainty of enrollments. The first is timing—what happens when budgeted enrollment expectations are not realized in fact? The second is complexity—what are the actual results of counting and projecting numbers of students in different ways?

If budgetary procedures prescribe, for example, a student/faculty ratio of 17/1 at some point in time, the dollars represented by the ratio should reflect the actual number of students during the budget period. In most systems, central administration monitors campus enrollments and reallocates resources accordingly. This is not an easy task, however, even if system-wide enrollments are exactly projected. As one budget officer said, "At first, I always relax when compensating errors have produced the correct enrollment. Then the calls start coming in. The campuses with increased enrollment really need the money now. Those who are losers in the fall are certain that spring enrollment will bring them up to their projection."

The problem of adjusting dollars to students is generally met by requiring the campus to institute savings to reflect decreased enrollment. In the two California systems, if actual systemwide enrollment falls two percent or more below budgeted enrollment, excess funds are "unallocated" by the state. In the University of North Carolina, central administration employs a similar two percent rule in the allocation of campus budgets. In both states, funds which are "unallocated" or "saved" because of enrollment declines are less than the average cost per student used for enrollment increases. In general, budgetary formulas provide support for each additional student in excess of the actual marginal cost. While enrollments are growing, the difference is a source of fiscal flexibility. But when enrollments decline, use of the same formula will accentuate or accelerate the impact of decline because the increment of formula support withdrawn is greater than the marginal savings. Adjustment may be particularly great for graduate education where formula support was deliberately designed to encourage growth (Breneman, 1975). In practice, however, formulas are not applied mechanically. They are rarely fully funded in times of growth and are often adjusted—as in California and North Carolina—in the event of enrollment declines.

In North Carolina, the amount withdrawn is, in substance, only instructional salaries and library costs attributable to enrollment. In the California State University and Colleges, the amount is negotiated but approximates the North Carolina figure. In these and in most other systems, the state allows a year for the system and its campuses to adjust to the lower enrollment.

The University of Texas does not utilize projected enrollment targets. Like other public campuses in Texas, it is budgeted on the basis of actual enrollment of the prior year in a biennial budget process. The state budget allocates funds specifically to each campus. Campuses are required to adjust to enrollment shortfalls during the biennium based on complex statewide formulas used for fund acquisition. The two-year adjustment period allowed is the most liberal among the seven states in the study. Although not designed to do so, if the occasion arises Texas procedures permit an individual campus to have more time to readjust resources to fewer students.

Time for adjustment is essential. In the Universities of California and Missouri, for example, individual campuses had substantial enrollment declines, but time and circumstance permitted each system to take steps to ensure that tenured faculty were not laid off. In contrast, the difficulties faced by the University of Wisconsin are in part attributable to the inflexibility of budget procedures. In addition, the University of Wisconsin is the only system which faced overall enrollment decline and simultaneous base budget reduction. The conjunction of all of these factors caused layoffs. A university budget memorandum comments on the cumulative impact of these elements and notes the substantial amounts involved (University of Wisconsin, 1973c):

> Yet, for many [campuses], the juxtaposition of requirements for 100 percent adjustment to both enrollment shortfall *and* revised enrollments by July 1, 1974 and the negative features of a second year budget which already called for additional productivity savings, relinquishing of transitional funding and possible loss of federal funding offset support places them in an extremely disadvantageous position. . . .
>
> The university system's retrenchment problems can be seen by the fact that *five* university cluster campuses face an *unanticipated 1974-75 budget problem of $−3,439,000* in addition to a budgeted reduction of $−1,490,000. This represents the cumulative effect of enrollment changes, but does not reflect 1974-75 productivity savings nor the possibility of Level III funding.

The problem in the University of Wisconsin is simple to state but difficult to resolve. Academic programs and faculty assignments are based on enrollment projections. If fewer students show up than have been projected, budgeted funds must be returned to the state—half in November, half the following spring. In addition, the base budget reductions in 1973-74 made layoffs inevitable. One-time transitional funding from the state to permit one-year notices to tenured faculty provided partial relief, but the necessity for such emergency measures was a result of inflexible budget procedures.

Complexity is the term used for the continuum of formulas and guidelines which determine how students are counted for the purpose of budgetary allocation. The simple extreme of this continuum—student headcount—matches a tangible body with a single number (though difficult questions of when to count the bodies are always present). For budgetary purposes, student headcount is translated into full-time-equivalent (FTE) students by all systems. In most instances, FTE students are then divided by level of student or level of instruction. The Universities of North Carolina and Wisconsin also count students by the character of campus on which they are located. In the University of Wisconsin, as in the University of Texas, discipline categories add to the complexity. Ways of counting students differ according to purpose—for example, the University of California projects students by headcount for planning purposes and then translates such projections into FTE students for annual budgeting.

Over time, new and more sophisticated counting procedures have developed, and comparison of enrollment for one year with that for another may depend on intimate familiarity with technical change. The extent of systemwide concern over methods of counting students varies as greatly as the methods themselves, but generally depends on the role central administration plays in the allocation of resources among campuses and in the distribution or balance of programs within them. At one extreme is the University of Texas, where complex statewide formulas allocate funds directly to campuses, with no system authority to shift funds among them. Future internal shifts in student distribution, however, may change the role of the system. State funding for master's level instruction is two to three times greater than for undergraduate instruction, and seven to nine times greater for doctoral instruction, depending on the discipline. Major declines of doctoral students could substantially reduce state funding, even with a constant overall campus enrollment, perhaps to the extent that system concern would be required. The formula system has served the university well during its period of expansion, but it may not provide needed flexibility should growth cease—a possibility, even in Texas.

The University of Illinois budget request, based on program needs and projected costs, is subject to coordinating agency review and recommendations (generally based on conventional assumptions about the higher cost of graduate instruction). The University of Illinois plans phased reduction of the total enrollment of Chicago Circle, but with a major shift in program emphasis from undergraduate to graduate instruction. University administrators hope that higher support for graduate instruction will offset the planned drop in undergraduate enroll-ment to keep real budgets the same, but maintaining the bal-ance may prove difficult to implement.

In California, state funding is generally incremental, start-ing from the base of the prior year. After adjustments to the base, enrollment changes are reflected by additions or subtrac-tions to historical systemwide student/faculty ratios. Current procedures replace more structured, yet separate, procedures for the two California systems. Sharply contrasting opinions between the two systems as to the acceptability of current state practice reflect historical differences in funding levels and fiscal flexibility, as well as differences in academic programs and mis-sions.

In the California State University and Colleges system, budget administrators disagree with the current aggregated stu-dent/faculty ratio approach. They are urging state officials to adopt more detailed procedures that recognize cost differentials by student level, and possibly by discipline. The problem faced by State University is one of internal changes in student de-mand. The apparent shift in student interest in 1974 from lib-eral arts disciplines such as history to more career-oriented programs such as nursing poses a funding dilemma. An overall systemwide student/faculty ratio of 18/1 encompasses, for example, ratios of 35/1 in history departments and 7/1 in nurs-ing programs. Current budgetary procedures do not recognize the need for the funding of two additional faculty positions when 22 students choose nursing over history.

In the University of California, on the other hand, while budget administrators clearly wish to improve the overall stu-dent/faculty ratio, they are much less critical of the procedure itself. Unlike the California State University and Colleges, the University of California was funded in the past by a weighted student/faculty ratio and support level expressly developed to encourage and provide more state funds for graduate instruc-tion. Even though only partially funded when operative, this practice has left a legacy of a substantially higher level of fund-ing than that of State University, admittedly in part for more expensive graduate programs. As the now defunct separate formulas were developed in the 1950s and 1960s, State University was subject to detailed budgetary controls from which the University of California was free. The prospect of the state drawing finer distinctions among academic programs has little appeal to administrators of either system. Administrators of California State University, however, find that the legacy of budgetary inflexibility requires them to urge such a course.

The timing and complexity of technical budgetary practices were minor irritants in the past, with little glamor except for those who worked with them on a daily basis. In 1975, however, both factors have major impact on the ability of multicampus systems to adjust to shifting student numbers and demands.

Flexibility

In general, a multicampus system can exercise fiscal flexibility either through regular budgetary procedures or through funds which are particularly generated or provided for that purpose. Transfer of funds is one regular budgetary procedure that permits flexibility. Of the nine multicampus systems under study, only the University of Texas does not have authority to transfer funds among campuses, at least within major programs. In the other eight systems, in some instances, approval of such transfers is required by state budget offices, but systemwide budget officers indicate little difficulty in obtaining such approval, and state budget authorities are reported to be sympathetic with the need for internal flexibility.

Recent changes in appropriation procedures for the State University of New York illustrate a commonality of interest between an executive budget office and a higher education institution. In 1972, the New York state comptroller, an elected official, challenged the single-line appropriations for each campus as not being legitimate line items within the meaning of state constitutional requirements for appropriations in that form. The challenge of the comptroller, backed by legislative fiscal committees, was opposed by the executive budget office and the State University. In part, the executive budget office recognized the need for budgetary flexibility in higher education. But preservation of gubernatorial authority was probably the more compelling reason. A compromise procedure currently requires appropriations in seven functional categories for each campus. State University administrators perceive the new procedures as a help to them in improving management practices at some campuses, but foresee operating difficulties (State University of New York, 1973, p. V-27):

> The new legislation may cause serious operational problems, since changing circumstances during the fiscal year may cause shortages and restrictions within functions. At the same time, it will require very careful and accurate functional planning and budgeting by each campus. The arrangements of earlier years tended to permit rather relaxed functional planning, and the operating summaries for some campuses at the end of the year showed little relationship to the functional plan presented at the beginning of the year. As a result of these new procedures, the University may have to make more use of the deficiency budget . . . to effect legitimate revisions in functional appropriations which exceed the 5 percent limitation. The flexibility to transfer funds in the past was one of the primary reasons the deficiency budget was little used.

Central administrative authority to move funds among programs and campuses may be valuable primarily "for putting out fires," as one system budget officer notes, but if carefully used may also be an effective tool for maintaining progress toward long range goals. In the Universities of California and Missouri, such flexibility prevented the layoff of tenured faculty at specific campuses with enrollment problems and resulting budget cuts.

Barring crisis situations, however, multicampus flexibility in budgeting is more likely to be seen in reallocation during the budget preparation cycle than in outright transfers within a budget year. For example, in North Carolina, reallocations merge almost imperceptibly into the budgetary process, and selective allocation of limited new money is equalizing distribution of funds among similar campuses.

More explicit reallocation occurs in the University of Wisconsin, where economy-of-scale curves relate instructional costs, academic support, and student services to campus size for 11 collegiate campuses. The objective is to bring all campuses within a fixed distance of the curve over a period of years through reallocation of campus base budgets. There is no intent to allocate funds precisely according to campus size, but rather to eliminate substantial and unjustifiable variations. The extent and timing of what might appear to be relatively mechanical budgetary adjustments in this process in fact represent considered academic judgment coupled with strong systemwide concern for campus autonomy.

In general, system administrators believe that reallocations among campuses and programs should be in the hands of the university, not the state budget office. Unquestionably, most of the states have competent budget staff who are as concerned about the welfare of higher education as system administrators. It does the state budget staff no injustice, however, to note that they serve political masters often impatient to reach political objectives. Daily concern for campus diversity and autonomy is a direct and specific responsibility of multicampus administrators. However understanding, governmental planning and budgeting agencies are required to have other priorities—particularly during times of fiscal stringency when such agencies act as watchdogs.

Common concerns of administrators at the University of Wisconsin and California State University and Colleges illustrate the distinction between academic and state administrators. Both systems have operating information processes of considerable sophistication. Detailed comparative data are provided to campuses as background for decisions based on a particular balance of programs at that campus. Data for other campuses are sometimes furnished but campuses are not always named. In both systems, administrators share the usual concern in higher education that state agencies will misuse these data. However, they also share a concern specific to the multicampus context: will the campuses make improper comparisons within the system, even against their own campus self-interest? Historical diversity among campuses can be lost as easily through conscious or unconscious misuse of data by campus administrators and faculty as by state agencies.

Although all but one system have the authority, substantial transfers of funds across campus boundaries have recently occurred in only two systems. In the University of Wisconsin, the combination of factors discussed earlier required the system to "borrow" $800,000 from the Madison and Milwaukee campuses for use elsewhere in the system. These two campuses, which had projected enrollment growth, absorbed portions of base budget reductions of other campuses facing enrollment declines. The transfer is said to have been motivated by three factors: realization by Madison administrators and faculty that they were part of a system and should help siblings in difficulty; political reality that indicated that the state might find ways to take the funds if they were not given voluntarily; and encouragement of the voluntary action by the central administration.

Whatever the motivations in Wisconsin, transfer of salary funds from the Urbana campus to the Medical Center and Chicago Circle campuses of the University of Illinois was clearly an act of the central administration. In the 1974-75 budget request, the university had made separate but equally compelling justifications for faculty salary increases for all three campuses. But the coordinating agency recommended and the legislature appropriated funds only in the amount requested for the Urbana campus. The central administration then utilized these funds for salary increases across all campuses. Urbana administrators and faculty resisted the loss of funds, and a complex compromise restored some of them. Despite what are described as "vigorous discussions" concerning the transfer, the issue is considered internal and did not involve state officials.

A second important budgetary procedure is the use of funds specifically intended to provide flexibility. Although state governments recognize the desirability of fiscal flexibility in the higher educational enterprise, direct appropriations of totally discretionary funds are rare. Where it does occur, recognition takes the form of appropriations for specific purposes to systemwide offices. Additional flexibility is permitted through the use of outside funds by the system or campuses. Marginal changes since 1970 in the nature and extent of discretionary fund appropriations are only peripherally related to enrollment and fiscal trends.

Only two multicampus systems have discretionary funds as such. In the City University of New York, the budget in 1974 allocated approximately $400,000 to the chancellor for special projects and for special needs. All expenditures from these two funds must be reported to the New York City budget authorities, and individual expenditures exceeding $50,000 and $75,000, respectively, are subject to preaudit review.

In the University of Texas, the Available University Fund is a major source of flexibility, but use is restricted to educational and general activities, largely at the Austin campus. The state constitution defines the fund as income from the Permanent Fund, which consists of large oil and gas properties owned and managed by the university. Although constitutionally based, some believe state officials could offset the income against state appropriated funds in the regular university budget. To date, however, this prospect has not been raised.

More commonly, state appropriations for academic programs at a systemwide level are limited to specific programs. The limitation may be relatively narrow, as is the case of graduate fellowship funds in the State University of New York (1974a, p. 481): "An appropriation of $500,000 is recommended for graduate fellowships, to be controlled by the university's central administration and distributed to program areas of specific need. The funds would not be used to expand graduate enrollments but to attract students with high ability and those studying in areas of manpower shortage or public concern." On the other hand, the appropriation may be quite broad, as in funding for curricular development at the University of Wisconsin, or in support of innovative programs at the California State University and Colleges: "For support of innovative projects, Trustees of the California State University and

Colleges, in addition to and augmentation of Item 359. . . . $1,401,248" (State of California, 1974a, p. 112).

Whether state appropriated funds are so broadly worded as to be truly discretionary contingency funds, or so narrowly circumscribed as to amount to specific appropriations, they are always highly visible, and vulnerable to fiscal stringency— ironically so, for in such times they are most needed.

With the exception of the University of Texas, the primary source of flexibility in multicampus systems and their campuses is indirect cost reimbursement, most of which derives from federally funded research grants and contracts. Indirect cost reimbursement is intended to offset overhead costs arising from the use of university facilities for a particular project. Indirect costs are initially paid by the state, through the regular budgetary process, and in the case of the University of Texas, the state is completely repaid by an offset against the university budget. A compelling argument, however, is that but for the initiative of the institution in obtaining the research funds, there would be no reimbursement, and that total repayment would be a windfall to the state. In most multicampus universities, the latter reasoning is followed, and indirect cost reimbursement is shared.

Changes since 1970 in this area have been in the allocation of indirect cost reimbursement within the multicampus systems. The reasoning that leads to state sharing of these funds with a system also applies to redistribution within the system, for such funds are generated by the initiative of specific campuses, departments, and disciplines. Systemwide and campus administrators, of course, do not perceive retention of funds at their respective levels for reallocation as windfalls, since the funds remain within their organizations. Department chairmen do not find this distinction particularly compelling, however. Recent changes reflect ongoing attempts to reach a balance among three different options: retention of funds at the system level for internal reallocation without regard to the differential ability of campuses and disciplines to generate such funds; relatively unrestricted allocation to campuses to increase campuswide flexibility; and specific allocation to departments or disciplines in recognition of their initiative in generating the funds. Campus administrators and faculty believe that they have earned such funds and find support in many state budget offices.

In the California State University and Colleges and the University of North Carolina, indirect cost reimbursement traditionally has been returned to the campuses of origin. In both systems, only nominal amounts are retained for research administration in central offices. In the University of California, on the other hand, such funds are allocated by central administration and trustees, largely independent of where funds were earned, with a substantial portion used for student financial assistance throughout the system. In the University of Wisconsin, a similar pattern has been limited severely by the impact of enrollment and fiscal trends since 1969. In this system, indirect costs are now returned to the campus of origin. In part, this change is attributable to pressure from administrators and faculty at the Madison and Milwaukee campuses, which generate the vast bulk of outside research funds. Such pressures were increased when merger legislation created the possibility of wider sharing of funds among campuses of the former Wisconsin State University system.

The situation at the University of California is uncomplicated by organizational changes, and the impact of fiscal stringency upon use of indirect cost reimbursement is explicit. Substantial amounts are available for systemwide as opposed to campus purposes, but increasingly these are used for activities which used to be funded by the state. For example, in 1974-75, slightly over $2 million was allocated from university sources to fund systemwide programs deleted by the state from the budget request. Approximately $3.5 million was similarly allocated to campuses to cover unfunded budget requests. In contrast to these amounts, only $250,000 was retained for systemwide discretionary use, and $500,000 was distributed among nine campuses for the same purposes, substantially according to the research funding generated by each.

The value and use of grants from private funding agencies is another significant source of flexibility. Establishment of

Empire State College in the State University of New York was assisted by grants totaling $1 million from the Carnegie Corporation and the Ford Foundation. In the California State University and Colleges, the initial 1971 Carnegie Corporation grant of over $450,000 and positive campus response to it undoubtedly encouraged subsequent state funding for innovation.

Flexibility, whatever its source, may be in danger because of collective bargaining. Academic personnel constitute the largest single budgetary item. To the extent that faculty salaries and items covered under the term *related working conditions* are included in the bargaining contract, traditional budgeting practice is restricted. Of the nine multicampus systems, only faculty at two—City and State Universities of New York—are presently covered by collective bargaining agreements; five expect increased union activity; and two—the Universities of North Carolina and Texas—remain relatively untouched.

In the City University of New York, budgetary implications of collective bargaining are clouded by broader issues of relationships between city and state. One issue, however, is clearly emerging: although the state funds 50 percent of the City University budget, it has no role in the negotiations which determine faculty salaries. Yet these salaries are substantially higher than those fixed by the State University collective bargaining agreement, which is directly negotiated by the state. New York City is unable to sustain this differential without state assistance, but the state may become unwilling to provide assistance without participation in the negotiating process.

Whatever the outcome, at either city or state level, the budget for the two New York systems will be increasingly dominated by the bargaining contract. If budgetary flexibility in resource allocation is a critical element of effective administration, this flexibility will have to be sought in the contract as well as in the budget. That union representatives will be as sympathetic to this need as state executive agencies is doubtful. Yet the issue goes to the heart of multicampus governance.

A similar question raised in all multicampus systems is whether salaries and salary increments (cost-of-living, merit, and the like) are separately budgeted or integrated into a general academic support category without differentiation. In the State University of New York, for example, campuses can either pay higher salaries to fewer faculty members or add staff and hold the line on salaries (although this option does not apply to the negotiated across-the-board cost-of living increase in the current contract). In other systems in which student/faculty ratios provide the basis for the budget and position control exists, as in California, budgetary adjustments take place without reference to separately budgeted salary increase funds. Flexibility increases to the extent that commingling is permissible. But with growing attention to salaries under pressures of inflation and collective bargaining, flexibility may be sharply reduced.

State Intervention

University budgets are clearly an appropriate channel for use by governors and legislators to express public policy. Enrollment and fiscal trends, for example, have state policy implications and should be reflected in budgetary practices. But budgets can also be an inappropriate channel by which officials intervene in internal system governance. Aside from the direct relationship between enrollment and funding formulas and guidelines, however, there is surprisingly little evidence that either enrollment trends or fiscal stringency, as such, have increased state intervention in university affairs through budgets. Instead, greater intervention is variously attributed to the increasing size and competency of executive and legislative staff, to conflicts between the governor and the legislature, or to a legacy of distrust from the days of student disruption.

In three systems—the Universities of Illinois, Missouri, and North Carolina—recent examples of direct political interference have been relatively limited despite the increasing size and sophistication of governmental budgetary staff. System administrators are not immune to special probes by legislators and legislative committees, but these have been few in number and usually informal. In the University of Illinois, for example, administrators try to determine the precise issue of concern to the legislator and to reach an agreement with him on the exact nature and extent of the information needed for response. Such understandings can limit the time and cost of responding as well as avoid an unsatisfactory response.

In Wisconsin, the budgetary process is characterized by explicit statements of issues, alternatives, and reasons for decisions at all levels from campuses to systemwide offices and state agencies. Extensive formal documentation is supplemented by informal contacts. Two aspects of this relationship are important in a discussion of state budgetary controls. First, wide and largely public sharing of information about budgetary analyses and resulting negotiations soften the impact of state control. Although systemwide administrators are well aware that the legislature is overstepping the conventional boundary between legislative and system prerogatives, they accept such intervention as an unwelcome but perhaps necessary concomitant of an overall constructive budgetary relationship.

However, the second major aspect of the relationship between university and state in Wisconsin is the administrative burden necessary to maintain it. In 1973, for example, the university was required to respond to seven legislatively mandated studies and three required by the governor—all within five or six months. No single inquiry was unreasonable but responding to all of them imposed an enormous burden. While the maintenance of an open relationship with the state is burdensome to the University of Wisconsin, it is not generally perceived as unwarranted interference with academic administration.

New York is an outstanding example of a state in which the governor plays the major role in the budgetary process. During the administration of Governor Rockefeller, the State University of New York clearly benefited from his interest in its growth and welfare. Even then, the legislature was restive with a relatively minor role, and with subsequent changes of administration is attempting to assert a stronger one. The State University is in the middle of this broader struggle for power, and the outcome is uncertain. We have already noted the revision in budget format to limit systemwide transfer of funds. Another—more minor—example of restriction is the way in which funds are budgeted for graduate fellowships to be distributed among campuses by State University central administration. The

assumption in the gubernatorial budget (as well as accepted
norms of governance) would allow the university this discretion,
but the legislature, in passing the 1974-75 budget, exercised its
own judgment (State of New York, 1974b): "The requested
number of new graduate fellowships is not justified. However,
in reviewing the allocation of existing fellowships and other
sources of graduate student support, it was found that inequi-
ties exist in the distribution of state-supported graduate assistance among the four university centers. For this reason, and to
express the Committees' concern for the development of high
quality graduate programs at the State University, funding is
provided to establish fifty new graduate fellowships to be allocated to the university centers in the following manner: Albany,
5; Binghamton, 20; Buffalo, 10; Stony Brook, 15."

The California legislature has also made significant inroads
into the operations of the two state multicampus systems. As
but one of many possible examples, in the conference committee report which accompanied the 1974-75 budget, the California legislature mandated all but the administrative details for
affirmative action programs at California State University and
Colleges and the University of California, requiring a full-time
affirmative action officer at system and campus levels and specifying job qualifications and responsibilities. The legislature
required numerous comprehensive and detailed studies to be
undertaken, and further directed each system and campus to
establish separate advisory committees to deal with student,
staff, and faculty affirmative action programs.

The issue raised by such legislative action is not the good
intent of either the legislature or the constituencies to whom it
is responding, but whether the budgetary process should be
used to enunciate not merely policy but detailed procedural
guidelines. The State University rural Stanislaus campus with
2,200 students, and UCLA with 30,000 students, assuredly have
the same objectives in their affirmative action programs. It is
highly improbable, however, that identical procedures can or
should be applied in reaching these objectives. Indeed, by requiring identical practices at vastly different campuses in quite
different educational systems, the California legislature may

effectively limit the flexibility that each must have to meet moral and legal obligations.

Although the state budget for a multicampus system is a proper and important vehicle for the expression of state policy, it is nevertheless a fiscal document. Practices and procedures designed to resolve fiscal issues may be ill suited for consideration of substantive ones. Although legislative conference committees are traditional and necessary for the resolution of differences between houses on fiscal matters, such committees may overreach proper roles when deciding broad educational policy issues or narrow program questions. How and where such substantive issues should be resolved are questions that must be answered within the political context of each state. But whatever the arena, it should be one which allows and encourages the full participation of the affected institutions, the executive branch of state government where appropriate, and the general public.

5

Strategies for
Program Development

Traditional concepts of higher education include full-time campus residency at one campus, face-to-face contact between instructor and student in lectures or laboratories, and students between 18 and 24 years of age. If the quality of instruction could be held constant, then departure from traditional methods could also mean freedom from traditional cost and physical limitations. Instruction through closed-circuit television, computer-assisted programs, video cassettes, or in open universities in part-time programs, or in programs drawing upon the resources of two or more campuses might permit enrollment of different students (or the same students reached through different means), possibly for less cost and with better results.

The benefits of additional students and lower costs seem clear. The multicampus system would seem to enjoy several advantages in the search for new approaches: it can be a source of financial and technical support for campuses, but limit risk to one campus; it can be an objective judge of experimental success or failure; it has interior lines of communication to transfer successful programs to a wider—perhaps captive—audience. With physical and educational resources widely scattered across a state, a multicampus system can reach a statewide nonresident student body and it can more readily develop programs drawing upon broad resources of more than one campus.

Five years ago, we found "isolated examples of joint instructional and degree programs involving faculty and facilities
from more than one campus" (Lee and Bowen, 1971, p. 244),
but urged that more needed to be done in this area: "Far more
attention should be given to systemwide programs that capitalize upon the strengths and needs of several campuses. . . . The
opportunity for the multicampus university to meet this challenge is immense. Drawing upon resources denied to a single
campus, able to implement programs in a manner beyond the
ability of a coordinating agency, the institutional vehicle seems
almost ready-made. Internal acceptability, given the conservatism of the academic toward his own affairs, and external support, given the demands of competing public expenditures, will
not come easily. Nevertheless the effort must be made" (Lee
and Bowen, 1971, p. 452).

As discussed in preceding chapters, multicampus systems
have assumed a more active role in academic planning and program review in response to actual or declining enrollment and
increasing fiscal stringency. To be sure, system activity in these
areas largely depends upon campus initiative and often entails
disapproval of such initiative. Major critics of higher education
systems are genuinely concerned that another bureaucratic layer
stifles the diversity and creativeness of campuses (see, for example, Newman and others, 1971, pp. 23-27). However, this is not
a clear and present concern in the nine multicampus systems
under study. To the contrary, planning and program review
procedures and structures explicitly protect campus autonomy
and initiative. Indeed, if the only multicampus role were that of
ensuring balanced resource and program allocation among campuses, both campuses and states would be well served by these
nine systems.

However, more is required. The recent increase in planning
and program review activity has led most systems to take greater interest in the substance of academic programs—in what is
taught, how, where, and by whom—as well as in nontraditional
students, better mobilization of resources of several campuses,
and new modes of teaching. Our discussion of innovative academic programs identifies three types of programs: nontradi-

tional programs, defined as off-campus or part-time instruction (or both); multicampus programs, administered by central administration, a campus, or a regional consortium; and innovative and experimental programs, for both traditional and part-time students at system or campus level (or both).

This classification is a framework for discussion, not an organizational construct presently within universities. For example, the City University of New York baccalaureate degree, discussed as a multicampus program, is also nontraditional in part, and certainly is innovative. And the meaning of the term *traditional* is always specific to a multicampus system: a seemingly modest policy change allowing part-time students to pay partial fees within the University of California was quite nontraditional in that system.

We stress again that our focus is on systemwide activity not individual campus programs. The heart of innovation and experimentation is in the classroom, not in the central administration, and intercampus cooperation can take place in and out of multicampus systems. Much is going on within each campus of these large systems, just as in higher education generally, but this is beyond the purview of this inquiry. Our emphasis is on the role of the system in facilitating and monitoring new program strategies. This role may be limited, but it is often critical.

Nontraditional Programs

As might be suspected, interest in nontraditional programs is extremely varied: three of the systems are actively engaged in external degree programs, though in substantially different ways, three are investigating such programs with varying degrees of urgency, and three are not actively concerned with the issue. The most visible nontraditional degree program is that of the State University of New York's Empire State College, described in the current State University master plan (1972b, p. 45) as a "noncampus college serving young people and adults who are able to pursue college study without the conventional structures of campus and classroom instruction. Empire State Learning Centers, staffed by a dean and a group of faculty members, will be developed in each of the university's four major regions of the state.

As of April 1974, over 400 associate and baccalaureate degrees had been awarded, and Empire State College administrative and academic personnel were housed on five State University campuses in addition to the four regional centers. Empire State College is treated as if it were a campus within the organizational structure. State University administrators look on Empire State as a resource available to assist them when residential campuses lack resources or incentive, expecting it, for example, to take an active role in proposed plans for prisoner education and to participate in a consortium which offers instruction on an Indian reservation.

Empire State was not created to bolster faltering enrollments. By systemwide administrators at least, it is not seen as competing with residential campuses for students, but as a model for these campuses in showing the potential clientele that could be reached through off-campus instruction. Empire State was among the first alternatives to traditional education in the United States, is undoubtedly the most visible, and in contrast with similar programs in the two California systems, appears to have a permanent structure.

The role of nontraditional education in California is both flexible and uncertain in 1975. Prior to the present concern over enrollments, both the University of California and California State University and Colleges initiated quite different projects in the early 1970s in response to legislative encouragement.

The Extended University of the University of California is intended to experiment with means for meeting educational needs of adults unable to attend campus degree programs on a full-time basis. Started as a three-year pilot program with internal funding in the fall of 1972, state support was available for the next two years. The extent of state support is in doubt, however, as the three-year period draws to a close in 1975. Unlike Empire State College, the extended university is not a separate operating unit, but rather a review and funding agency for campus-initiated programs that is coordinated by a systemwide officer under general system guidelines. Only upper-division and master's degree programs are offered. While the three-year pilot study has clarified a number of administrative and academic issues, many of the latter remain unresolved, as indicated in a report to the governing board (University of California, 1974a, p. 19):

> Extended University was to establish regional and statewide academic programs, where appropriate, using the academic resources of one or more campuses for its accomplishment. To date, appropriate policy and structure for significant regional and statewide programing have not yet been devised. A number of barriers remain. These include campus residence requirements, reluctance of campuses to transfer courses and use of faculty jointly. Clearly, it is structurally easier for the faculty of a single campus to offer an academic program throughout the state or a given region than it is to combine the programs of two or more campuses, which might yield a better program than any one of its members.
>
> In addition to the necessity to build structures for intercampus cooperation, cooperative arrangements need to be formed with other segments of California postsecondary education—both public and private. Many of these institutions also have begun to offer academic degree programs to individuals at locations which are remote from campuses. A significant cost savings as well as program enrichment can be obtained by cooperative efforts at those remote locations.

In 1971, California State University and Colleges undertook a broad, three-year program called New Approaches to Higher Education. One of the major thrusts of the program was the appointment of a Commission on External Degree Programs made up of faculty and administrators. Although reporting directly to the system chief executive, the commission has been administratively headquartered at the campus of its chairman.

Among its many activities, the commission has developed procedures for parallel instruction under which a single student who cannot attend courses is able to obtain credit from an individual professor. Curriculum concords have been devised for transfer and acceptance of credit among the 19 campuses of the system. Ongoing evening programs have been promoted (which have long met many of the less glamorous objectives of nontraditional education in many institutions). Procedures for offering external degrees have been established; these differ from those of the University of California in that program approval is directly in the hands of the commission rather than individual campuses. This provides an alternative channel of review and the chance for greater systemwide leverage. The major accomplishment of the commission, however, is the establishment of the Consortium of California State University and Colleges as a separate entity to grant external degrees.

The Consortium is an operational unit but unlike Empire State College does not have faculty of its own. The Consortium offers instruction through campus faculty and acts as a coordinating, credit-awarding, degree-granting body. The organization is complex, but deserves description as an effective effort to utilize resources of several campuses.

Although formally only advisory, the de facto policy board for the Consortium is a nine-member committee of the statewide faculty senate, with six members appointed by the senate itself and three appointed by the system executive. An operating director of the Consortium is part of central administration, but responsibility for each program is in the hands of an academic program committee consisting of faculty from at least five campuses. In substance, these committees are systemwide departments under whose auspices the program operates. Nine such committees were functioning in 1974.

In the field of public administration, for example, 13 campuses cooperatively offer intensive all-day seminars and individual tutorial projects at four sites throughout the state. At the San Francisco site, instruction by faculty from five campuses is administered by a regional coordinator. Student fees are determined on the same basis used for extension programs, and the campus from which a faculty member is drawn receives budgetary credit for his extension teaching. The Consortium gives credits toward and awards a degree. Programs offered by the Consortium need not be in participating campus master plans, and systemwide approval is required only once for the Consortium program itself (not for each of 13 campuses).

The future of the nontraditional programs of both California systems may be clouded by legislative interest in creating a separate organization (a so-called "fourth segment" of higher education) with responsibility for external degrees. Such an organization was recommended by a legislative committee studying the master plan in 1973, and a feasibility study was mandated. The request for proposals for the feasibility study (State of California, 1974b, p. 1) expressed concern over both access and instructional delivery systems, and concluded that "the emerging educational programs which partially address these two concerns are developing in a fragmented and uncoordinated manner."

The feasibility study will be completed in June 1975. Whatever its recommendations, the two systems are attempting to coordinate their extended degree programs. A major example of coordination is the Ventura Learning Center, dedicated in late 1974. The Center came into being when the University of California required rented space in Ventura for continuing education programs. Situated in a region without a nearby four-year institution, the Center now offers both extended degree and extension programs sponsored by the two multicampus systems. A resident director is selected and paid by both systems, and other costs are also equally shared.

Aside from Empire State College and the two programs in California, only the University of Wisconsin has a firm plan for offering external degrees. It proposes a unit to be known as Regents' Statewide University to be headed by an operating executive officer reporting through a provost for outreach. The latter also has responsibility for the existing university extension and the 14-campus two-year center system, each with its own executive head. The program has been endorsed by the legislature but not funded. In general, it proposes programs similar to those offered by California State University and Colleges. All University of Wisconsin campuses would be physical bases for program offerings, but the faculty would be organized on a systemwide basis.

Little is happening in nontraditional education in the other five multicampus systems. In New York City, indeed, little more could be done: there are few locations which are not convenient to some City University campus, there is a long tradition of part-time and evening work, and the recently established systemwide baccalaureate degree allows off-campus work. In the University of Missouri, a faculty committee appointed by the system executive recommended a largely campus-based program along the lines of the Extended University of California, but in early 1975, the recommendations had not been acted upon. At the University of North Carolina, discussions of nontraditional offerings were initiated in 1974 and a study undertaken with the help of an outside grant. At the University of Texas, the higher priority is building new campuses to accommodate previously unserved but traditional residential students. In Illinois, considerations at a statewide level are still unresolved.

Although concerns over declining enrollment were not factors in the establishment of the three nontraditional programs in California and New York, these programs are nevertheless relevant to current enrollment trends. Nontraditional education allows a system to meet new demands without major long term commitments in faculty or physical facilities and can serve as a model for existing campuses wishing to break the lockstep of traditional offerings. Even though "the excitement of investing in open learning programs has subsided," as pointedly noted in a 1974 study by University of Missouri faculty, nontraditional education is here to stay, and the extent of flexibility afforded any institution is significantly increased in the multicampus context. It is too early to choose among models outlined above, but certainly all should be carefully analyzed by institutions considering such programs.

Multicampus Programs

In the past five years, the number of academic programs explicitly designed to encompass more than one campus has increased substantially. The increase is attributable partially to current enrollment and fiscal problems. In addition, joint or cooperative programs increase educational options when a critical mass of students and faculty exist within a geographic area, although not at a single campus.

Multicampus programs generally fall into three categories: systemwide programs which involve all campuses and require substantial central administration concern; regional programs which encompass campuses in specifically designated areas of the state; and specific programs—usually joint programs between two campuses—which are a residual category. Agricultural experiment stations and agricultural and general extension activities, long a part of the higher education scene, are excluded from this discussion.

Systemwide programs. Every multicampus university has systemwide academic programs which require academic work at more than one campus, encourage all campuses to utilize the specialized library and research facilities of one campus, and administer a systemwide laboratory, observatory, or the like. Many of these programs were initiated in the past for reasons other than enrollment constraints. Other recently established systemwide programs have resulted much more explicitly from current incentives to marshall and conserve resources.

City University of New York affords two illustrations: the advanced graduate work, offered by a separate organizational entity since 1961, and the CUNY Baccalaureate Program, established in 1972. Both are excellent lenses for examination of the impact of the changing environment of the 1970s on multicampus operations, although neither was established with current enrollment and fiscal trends in mind.

The graduate center, with its separate campus and administration, offers instruction both through its own faculty and through faculty drawn from campuses of City University. Although successful as an institution, the center has yet to resolve two issues which will arise whenever academic programs are offered apart from regular campuses. The first is the emphasis and direction of the programs themselves. On the one hand, the graduate school might limit offerings to programs of nationally recognized quality, taking advantage of its unique urban location to develop a highly specialized focus. On the other hand, it might concentrate on service to the undergraduate campuses by providing options for students and by assisting campuses in attracting faculty across a broad array of representative graduate programs. The choice is not an obvious one between "excellence" and "mediocrity," but a more difficult and subtle one between different dimensions of quality.

The second and related issue is the organization of campus faculty for instruction at the graduate school. For example, some 350 faculty members teach history in City University. Of these, 50 are designated as doctoral faculty and may teach at the graduate school. However, enrollment and physical space limit the number who can teach to 12 each semester or 24 each year. If all doctoral faculty teach on an equal basis, an individual faculty member can teach a course only once every five semesters. This lack of continuity appeals to neither faculty nor students, but the selection of a core faculty to ensure program continuity creates an in-group isolated from their home campuses. The search for a viable middle ground on these issues continues.

The CUNY Baccalaureate Program is the second City University illustration. The program permits a student, with the guidance and approval of a faculty committee, to develop a study plan which must include at least 90 credits of classroom work, but which may be taken at one or more City University campuses. Additional credit units may be earned through off-campus or, in the terms of the program, nonclassroom work. Applicants are carefully screened, and enrollment is limited to ensure that only students who have clear educational objectives are admitted.

The CUNY Baccalaureate Program also offers lessons for other multicampus systems. First, mere mechanics of keeping track of students across campuses require an adequate central staff. Second, registration procedures must avoid arbitrary barriers against student mobility. Third, care must be taken to avoid faculty misunderstanding of program goals. Finally, guidelines for faculty time and compensation should be clearly outlined. None of the faculty serving as advisors or coordinators in the CUNY program receives either added compensation or released time. The collective bargaining agent filed a grievance against the governing board claiming that such faculty were entitled to back pay as well as current compensation. The grievance was dismissed on the grounds that none of the faculty was in fact aggrieved. While this result speaks well for the dedication of City University faculty who teach in the program, guidelines would have avoided controversy.

At the opposite organizational extreme from City University graduate school, the University of Missouri proposes to offer graduate programs through systemwide—as opposed to campus—degrees but without a separate school or center. Briefly, doctoral instruction will be offered by the university doctoral faculty, to be selected by an elected university council. Membership in the campus graduate faculty will not automatically confer membership in the university doctoral faculty whose qualifications will be set by systemwide criteria.

Each doctoral program will be under the overall supervision of a discipline or sector coordinating committee made up of representatives of the university doctoral faculty elected from each relevant campus. A major responsibility of these coordinating committees is to bring together resources of four campuses by doing the following (University of Missouri, 1973c, p. 4):

> (1) Coordinating and cooperating in such areas as: maximum utilization of both faculty and equipment; student recruitment, admission, and transfer requirements; listing of qualified advisers; reporting of research activity; uniformity of requirements for identical degrees; conduct of seminars and course offerings; and cross-involvement in committee structure.
> (2) Maintaining review of the doctoral program, with particular attention to the need for change and quality improvement.
> (3) Implementing needed academic changes within their own areas of responsibility and existing campus administrative structures.

The plan to offer university degrees through the cooperative effort of faculty drawn from all campuses is ambitious. It
will confront the same dilemmas of the City University program: to what extent, if at all, should cooperative programs
develop specialized goals and missions separate from those of
campuses? How will faculty time be allocated?

In 1970, the probabilities of success for such a cooperative
degree program would have been bleak, but in 1975 the outlook
is more promising. The long process of developing the academic
plan required many Missouri faculty to take a broader multicampus view of their university. The view is clouded and controversial, to be sure, but necessities of the times may provide
the stimulus to make plans work.

System-directed multicampus instructional programs are
found in three other systems. In the State University of New
York, the Sea Grant Program is a more centralized operation
than similar but more campus-based programs in the Universities of California, North Carolina, and Wisconsin. Administrators at the State University of New York are convinced that
substantial participation from all campuses is possible only with
such centralization. Centralization is in fact limited to administration, while research, instructional, and service programs are
directed by campus faculty and by extension agents located at
several campuses.

The Sea Grant Program is an excellent example of multicampus cooperation. In particular, it broadens the experience of
faculty at four-year campuses who lack personal and professional research contacts. Firm guidelines for allocation of funds
ensure instructional support for both undergraduate and graduate students and fix limits on support of the systemwide Sea
Grant office.

The school of nursing at the University of Texas is another
organizational model for multicampus programs. Six branches
of the school in different locations operate under the direction
of a president located in the central administration. Like the
City University graduate school, this systemwide administrator
has responsibility for coordination, but unlike it, program offerings are located on campuses. This model may be limited to

professional education with fairly easily defined boundaries and standards. Even here, however, the need for sensitive handling of general-campus-nursing-school relationships is clear.

Regional programs. With major exceptions—the University of Missouri proposed systemwide doctoral program and the University of Texas nursing schools—most multicampus programs require campuses to be close enough to permit relatively easy interchange of faculty and students. In three multicampus universities, geographic regions are formally identified with varying degrees of structure. In the State University of New York, all campuses are assigned to one of four specific regions; in the University of Wisconsin, regional organization is fluid, overlapping, and developing; in the University of Texas, three north Texas campuses form a cooperative regional group, while maintaining separate administrative autonomy.

The most explicit and structured regional approach is in the State University of New York. Originally proposed in 1965, regional organization met with opposition from campus heads who were concerned about imposition of an additional layer of bureaucracy between them and system offices. Recent implementation has carefully avoided this criticism; administration is solely in the hands of committees made up of campus executives. Experience with the arrangement is described as "good, bad, and mixed." Although accepted by campuses both in concept and in operations, more is expected of regional organization than is presently being delivered.

In the State University, regionalism has four advantages. First, aspects of systemwide operations and programs overlarge in a centralized setting are reduced to manageable size. Examples include computer services, alumni activity, and selection of representatives to the statewide student assembly. Second, professional interchange is facilitated by bringing disciplinary groups of faculty together from different types of campuses, a proceeding too cumbersome for the university as a whole. Similarly, research involving specialists from several campuses is facilitated by regional organization; one region, for example, received a multicampus grant for a study in gerontology. Research experience and competency can be more readily shared between university centers and collegiate campuses in smaller regional groupings. Instructional coordination is the fourth advantage of regionalism, and the one which administrators in State University and elsewhere agree is frailest and most difficult to cultivate. An example is the theater semester in New York, which draws faculty from a university center, two four-year colleges, and four two-year colleges.

As with State University of New York, the University of Wisconsin regional thrust is only beginning to take shape. The review of master's programs discussed earlier raised the issue of the need for coordination to avoid unnecessary program duplication. The original plan to have two regional deans was altered when campus executives in the five-campus Eau Claire region convinced central administration that program review could be better conducted by a consortium. The regional dean approach, however, was followed in the three-campus Oshkosh area. Thus, a consortium and a regional dean are two different organization strategies with the same objectives, suggested by the mission of the Oshkosh campus (University of Wisconsin, 1974b, p. 13) to include "responsibility for initiating the mechanisms for on-going cooperative planning involving other system universities of the region and for providing post-baccalaureate educational opportunities needed by the citizens and agencies of the region as appropriate to the resources available to the universities."

The University of Texas has fewer governing functions associated with multicampus systems than any of the other eight in the study. Nevertheless, it affords an outstanding example of regional organization in the North Texas Council of Presidents in Dallas. Although executives of the three campuses— Dallas, Arlington, and the Health Science Center—have met with some regularity since 1969, only since 1972 have these meetings taken on a formal structure and expanded to initiate cooperative academic programs. Greater activity was originally defensive, much like the Eau Claire consortium. Concerned with the possibility of unnecessary program duplication presented by a proposal from one campus, the system executive suggested that he might have to appoint a regional administrator to coordinate

program offerings of all three. In response, presidential cooperation was swift, and results have exceeded, we suspect, the initial
expectations of all parties concerned.

At present, the three campus heads meet on a monthly
basis and, using campus funds, employ an executive secretary.
Their business officers likewise meet on a monthly basis. Some
12 faculty committees drawn from the three campuses coordinate specific programs and provide cross-campus professional
consultation. The three campus presidents also comprise the
policy board for the North Texas Computer Center, jointly
owned and operated by the three campuses under a single director. A school for allied health sciences has programs on the
three campuses, operating under a dean located at the Dallas
Health Science Center. Not all joint programs involve all three
campuses. Graduate work in humanities, for example, is offered
by only Dallas and Arlington. A recent external review of a
proposal for a three-campus mathematics program clearly indicates the benefits of the cooperation which has developed (University of Texas, undated, p. 2): "The pooling of resources in
faculty, course offerings, and library and plant facilities will
allow the strongest academic program at the least cost. The
Consulting Committee was impressed by the spirit of cooperation displayed by the representatives of these institutions. If
this attitude continues and leads to a variety of shared activities,
such as joint appointments between the institutions, combined
seminar and colloquium series, and the trading of faculty and
students for course work, research, and thesis advisement, then
the program will have a bright future as a truly integrated and
broadly based academic program."

Cooperation is not without rough spots. Although each of
the campus heads is searching for areas of mutual advantage,
each is also actively protecting the identity and autonomy of his
own campus in the absence of either a systemwide academic
plan or a consortium plan. The mutual confidence among the
three campuses and between campus and central administration
has developed without firm and definitive allocations of program responsibility. It is doubtful that more explicit *plans*
would have achieved more than the admittedly incremental

planning. The lesson is plain: in the present unstable world of higher education, a cooperative planning process is as important as a formal planning document, perhaps more so.

Specific programs. Each of the nine multicampus systems provides examples of specific joint-degree programs between campuses subject to varying guidance and encouragement from central administration. While all agree that establishment and operation of such programs is facilitated by inclusion of campuses within the multicampus structure, the system has generally played a relatively small role in their initiation.

In the University of North Carolina, for example, four campuses offer work at the Fort Bragg Graduate Center under the general coordination of an administrator located at the nearest four-year campus. Originally offering only extension work, present instruction is by regular faculty under the general budget. About half of the enrollment is military personnel, and the military pays additional costs of the off-campus instruction. The present program is responsive, at least in part, to the challenge that growing demands at Fort Bragg might be met by out-of-state institutions.

Intercampus cooperation in North Carolina is encouraged through systemwide councils in specific subject areas and in general areas such as research. Unlike somewhat similar efforts elsewhere, several of these councils have regular systemwide budget support. Greater systemwide activity in the future is expected for two reasons. First, as one administrator stated, "16 campuses instead of six have a greater opportunity to get into each others' hair"; second, university administrators must comply with the state desegregation plan required and monitored by HEW. Past informal cooperation between predominantly white and black campuses is becoming more explicit and structured, and will be subject to review in Washington. Joint offerings are being considered, but wide differences in the scholastic background of faculty and students will inhibit early development of many of these.

A different problem is found in the University of Illinois, where coordinating agency delays in approving new programs lor Chicago Circle campus have encouraged additions to graduate offerings through joint programs with Urbana and the Medical Center. Not everyone is satisfied with the compromises required, but most agree that progress has been made.

California State University and Colleges provides another illustration of ad hoc system encouragement and control over intercampus activity, albeit one which is demanding on the time and energy of the central staff. Degree programs in both geology and Russian are offered on a joint basis by State University campuses in the Los Angeles area. Each program was individually considered by system academic planning staff at the time of individual campus proposals. In the case of geology, only one campus, and in the case of Russian, none of the campuses, had sufficient students and faculty for single-campus programs. System administrators encouraged the joint programs and carefully set specific requirements to ensure that resources of more than one campus were in fact utilized. For example, in the three-campus geology program, each student must take at least one-fifth of his work on a campus other than that on which he is registered; class scheduling must be coordinated; and major equipment purchases must be centrally approved.

Most of these specific multicampus programs represent a shifting middle ground between campus-initiated programs and programs formally structured and planned centrally. The role of the central administration is by no means clear. Even in the University of North Carolina, where regular budget support is given to systemwide councils to encourage multicampus programs, campuses generally work out their own arrangements. Central administrators are sometimes concerned that multicampus programs are an easy way of avoiding difficult decisions of program allocation to a specific campus. Nevertheless, they do represent additional options for students.

Innovative and Experimental Programs

More often than not, the nontraditional and multicampus programs described above could also be classified as innovative and experimental. Yet treating innovative and experimental programs separately permits emphasis on an important example of systemwide leadership and action in the California State University and Colleges.

The major thrust for innovation came from the system executive's call for a new approach to higher education in 1971. Policy guidance is furnished by a joint administrative-faculty task force, and the program is directed by a special staff section in the central offices. "The establishment of a staff with special responsibilities in this area is based upon experience of other systems and institutions which have engaged in programs of innovation. This experience underlies the need to designate staff clearly responsible for program development, coordination and evaluation. Too many programs have begun in higher education, proved successful in themselves, only to be forgotten because no one was responsible for seeing that evaluation was completed, information disseminated, and successful activity implemented" (California State University and Colleges, 1973b, p. 30).

The broad objective of the program is to place more responsibility for learning upon the student, and it has proceeded in two related phases. The first was initiated in early 1971 when three campus proposals in response to the new approach were funded by a two-year grant of $450,000 from the Carnegie Corporation. The second and internally funded phase of the program started in early 1972 with the agreement of the governor's office to fund innovative projects in addition to those funded under the Carnegie grant. Over the 1972-75 period, over $3 million was provided in support of approximately 125 projects.

Some of the broad categories of funded projects reflect the wide scope of the program for innovation—for example, comprehensive/core examinations; credit by examination; dissemination of innovations; independent study; improvement of efficiency; reduction of attrition. Over the past three years, funding emphasis has shifted from smaller proposals with single-campus application to larger proposals with multicampus implications.

Of the many projects, the CSUC English Equivalency Test is often cited as especially successful. Experimentation with the Educational Testing Service CLEPS (college level examination programs general examinations) began in the fall of 1971. Considerable dissatisfaction was expressed with the "instant sophomores" resulting from the English examination, and, in 1972-73, under the auspices of the program for innovation, a systemwide English council surveyed existing examinations and ultimately designed the CSUC English Equivalency Test. The test is well publicized, established within the system, and also used by a number of community colleges. The cost of credit, awarded on the basis of the test in 1972-73, is estimated at approximately one-eighth that of regular classroom instruction.

Project proposals must contain provisions for evaluation within systemwide guidelines. Larger programs and those involving more than one campus require outside evaluation. Systemwide administrators at California State University and Colleges share the concerns of those in other multicampus systems about evaluation procedures. The absence of adequate qualitative output measures for traditional instruction makes it difficult to find control groups against which to assess innovation. This difficulty can be met by informed judgment, but such a substitution is less acceptable to funding agencies than quantitative cost evaluation. A similar problem exists in distinguishing between developmental and ongoing operational costs of innovative programs.

The extent of identifiable innovation in this system cannot be attributed to any single factor, but a most important contributing cause has undoubtedly been the leadership of the central administration. The chancellor's challenge to the academic lockstep of traditional programs and norms was also a challenge to a parallel administrative lockstep. Innovation was made a major priority, despite the high degree of organizational and procedural ambiguity necessary to achieve initially uncertain objectives. The initial support of the Carnegie Corporation and the continuing support of the state assuredly aided the program. However, successful instances of faculty effort within the program but without support indicate that, while dollars are desirable and useful, new ideas are not simply bought and sold in higher education.

Despite considerable exhortation, rhetoric, and even financial support, actual systemwide activity in the field of innovation and experimentation is notable for its absence in the other multicampus systems under study. In every system, central administrators pointed with pride to experimental programs initiated and supported at the campus level, but could rarely identify similar systemwide activity.

The State University of New York has a small systemwide staff with responsibilities in this area. However, annual state funding for innovative projects of approximately $500,000 in 1971 was terminated during a budget crisis and not restored. In 1975, emphasis is on improving undergraduate teaching and increasing its prestige.

A similar program in the University of California basically utilizes the system as a granting agency, without significant systemwide staff involvement. A state appropriation of $1 million earmarked for the improvement of undergraduate teaching, for example, was allocated to campuses essentially on the basis of undergraduate enrollments. While it is doubtful that new ideas are distributed in proportion to campus size, such distribution avoided the campus claims of unfair treatment raised in the California State University system. The dilemma is posed in an evaluation of the program (University of California, 1974d, p. 37): "Although there was some call for allocation of funds on the basis of the quality of projects submitted, rather than on a student enrollment basis, there was no consensus on how the essential characteristic called 'quality' should be determined, nor by whom, nor on how this could be accomplished without disturbing the values of campus autonomy."

There are, of course, specific innovative programs in every system that do not fall into the nontraditional or multicampus category. The professional development degree at the University of Missouri, the urban academy at the City University of New York, and the institute for undergraduate curricular reform at the University of North Carolina are all examples. We regret that we could not explore such programs in depth in the present study, for they are relevant: as enrollments and fiscal support stabilize, academic program flexibility will increasingly be related to alternative instructional methods.

6

Strategies for Faculty: Retrenchment and Renewal

The most visible problem in the unsteady state is the faculty. At its most extreme, the problem is seen in the dismissal or layoff of tenured persons confronted by empty classrooms. At its best, the problem is one of an aging professoriate, recruited in the 1950s and 1960s without adequate thought to the eventual profile of rank or age in 1980. While present in all higher education institutions, such situations pose special problems and opportunities for the multicampus system. These differ among systems, of course, depending on the relative similarity of campuses. But common to all is the possibility—short or long range—of collective bargaining by academics. Fiscal constraints require flexibility in the management of academic resources but also create barriers. How these two pressures are balanced with respect to faculty may do more than anything else to shape internal governance within the multicampus system.

Five short years ago, the dominant characteristics of academic personnel administration had been molded by a decade of expansion, of endless recruitment, and of the academic revolution with its emphasis on scholarship as the key criterion of appointment and promotion. The mood of the times and our concern for the future are reflected in our earlier study (Lee and Bowen, 1971, p. 275):

> The success of the multicampus university may be
> measured in many ways. A prime test would be the
> record of a system in recruiting and retaining a
> faculty and top-level administrators of high quality.

Expansion and recruitment are not the watchwords of the mid-
1970s. A few new campuses are starting up (only in Texas and
New York among the nine universities of this study), and scholarship remains the key to status in the academic marketplace.
But enrollment declines, program reductions, retrenchment, the
rights of both tenured and nontenured faculty in the face of
these, and the growing role of faculty unions—both in being and
in the process of creation—are now high on the agenda.

In this agenda, academic personnel policies and procedures
are influenced by three reasonably discrete factors. First, slowing enrollment growth is reflected in fewer new faculty members and, in some instances, enrollment declines result in faculty
layoffs. Second, deliberate curricular changes and shifting student demands create internal program volatility. Third, inflation
requires additional dollars to maintain real salary levels.

Enrollment

The number of faculty at campuses of a multicampus system
(like other public educational institutions) is specifically related
to the number of students; as noted previously, all nine multicampus universities are subject—explicitly or implicitly—to
budgetary student-faculty ratios. For faculty personnel planning, two aspects are critical: the scope of applicability of ratios
either to overall system enrollment or to that of specific campuses, and the timing of application of ratios.

The range of multicampus response to enrollment decline
is clearly limited if budgetary procedures tie faculty positions to
enrollment at a specific campus. In all systems, external and
internal constraints prevent major shifts of positions among
campuses, even though all except the University of Texas have
authority to do so. Administrators must maintain the legitimacy
and credibility of budgetary procedures with the legislature and
state budgetary agencies, and both the appearance and reality of

fair treatment are required within the system itself. Where these constraints are not too intense—as, for example, in the Universities of California and Illinois and in California State University and Colleges—shifting positions among campuses allows time for adjustment. Multicampus systems have responded in faculty policy and procedure to enrollment declines or stabilization at particular campuses either in terms of adjustment—prevention or slowdown of layoffs where time is available or crisis—the experience of the University of Wisconsin, where no time was available.

Policies and procedures to adjust the number of faculty to enrollment decline take three forms. First, procedures may be devised to ensure that processes of layoff or termination of faculty are fair. Second, distribution of faculty into tenured and nontenured or full-time and part-time classifications may be monitored or controlled. Third, systemwide resources may be marshalled for actual or prospective allocation to campuses in distress. Some aspect of such anticipatory procedures is found in all of the multicampus systems except the University of Illinois, which is relatively immune to the winds of shifting enrollment. The University of Illinois position as a capstone of higher education in the state is shared by other systems in the study, but with only two general campuses, this favored position is a tightly consolidated one.

In 1974-75, procedures for faculty layoff or dismissal were under development at the Universities of Texas and North Carolina and at California State University and Colleges. Emerging policies are generally based on recommended institutional regulations and the 1972 guidelines of the American Association of University Professors (AAUP), revised in November 1974. The AAUP (1974) revised regulations suggest that termination "may occur under extraordinary circumstances because of a demonstrably bona fide financial exigency which cannot be alleviated by less drastic means [or] as a result of bona fide formal discontinuance of a program or department of instruction." In both instances, the AAUP proposes, a faculty body should participate in deliberations; the faculty member should have the right to a hearing before a faculty committee; and the institution should make every effort to place the faculty member in another suitable position within the institution. With respect to cases of financial exigency, the right to return to the vacated position if funded, should remain with the faculty member for three years (unless the person involved declines reinstatement). "The burden will rest on the administration to prove the existence and extent of the condition [of financial exigency]," while cases involving program discontinuance "must reflect long range judgments [by the faculty] that the educational mission of the institution as a whole will be enhanced by the discontinuance." As with the 1972 guidelines, in cases of financial exigency, "the appointment of a faculty member with tenure will not be terminated in favor of retaining a faculty member without tenure." It is not clear at what level this last rule is to apply—program, department, college, or campus, but "judgments determining where within the overall academic program termination of appointments may occur involve considerations of educational policy, as well as of faculty status, and should therefore be the primary responsibility of the faculty or of an appropriate faculty body."

In the University of North Carolina system, pressures for a more uniform tenure policy are part of a broader concern with widely varying academic personnel policies of previously separately governed institutions. Systemwide interest is also a direct result of the fact that six campuses of the University of North Carolina lost budgeted positions (nontenured) because of enrollment decline from 1973 to 1975. In all but a few instances, attrition avoided actual layoffs. Within broad system guidelines, campuses are developing overall tenure regulations, and the central administration and governing board expect these to contain uniform language on layoff procedures. Uniformity will not be obtained without substantial negotiation with campuses, however. All faculty members are undoubtedly aware that funding, enrollment declines, and program shifts can place their jobs in jeopardy. But these are not pleasant thoughts, and faculty members are easily alarmed when administrators—particularly systemwide administrators—attempt to define such jeopardy in precise procedural terms.

The experience of Texas is instructive. In that state, the university was alerted to problems of declining enrollment by temporary declines at El Paso campus. Ad hoc crisis procedures resolved the El Paso problem, but central administration proposed to avoid future crises by adding dismissal provisions for bona fide fiscal exigency, decline in enrollment, or change in academic program to existing good cause provisions. After reviewing the system proposal, an Austin faculty committee suggested additional changes, derived mainly from AAUP guidelines, to strengthen the faculty role, but the Austin faculty as a whole rejected both the central administration proposal and that of its own committee. One faculty member "urged the faculty not to surrender in advance for fear that *somehow, sometime, someone* might be going to want to bring about a situation in which we must make that kind of capitulation" (University of Texas, 1974a). Free-floating faculty anxiety that "somehow, sometime, someone" in the administration will take advantage of them is probably found everywhere. In the University of Texas, such anxiety has delayed not only central administration attempts to institute orderly campus procedures, but also faculty efforts to ensure that procedures comply with AAUP guidelines and entail substantial faculty participation.

In California State University and Colleges, a joint faculty and administrative task force report (1974b) on steady state staffing is of particular interest. The report was deliberately limited to the immediate issue of layoffs, deferring the exploration of long term matters, such as early retirement, until a later date. The proposals of this task force are clearly a step in the direction of relating specific procedures to specific causes. The report notes two general conditions under which it will be considered mandatory to reduce the number of budgeted faculty positions: "(1) when a deliberate process of *curricular revision or program review* yields the conclusion that the number of faculty positions allocated to a discipline must be reduced or an entire program phased out, or (2) when *loss of enrollment* within an institution or discipline mandates a reduction."

The task force Report does not attempt to draw detailed systemwide procedures for the two causes for faculty reduction.

Instead, it suggests broad policies, supplementing these with specific checkpoints against which campus procedures could be measured.

With respect to faculty reduction caused by programmatic change, the task force recommends that campus procedures be integrated with campus responsibilities for academic planning and program review. Following the general thrust of the AAUP guidelines, the Report suggests that final program recommendations be made by a committee at least half of whose members are "nonadministrative" faculty, and that representatives of the discipline in question participate. Procedures clearly emphasize the viability of the educational program, not whether there are too many faculty or too few students, although these latter questions are a part of every program review.

In contrast, proposed procedures relating to enrollment decline are quite specific. Briefly, a committee at least one-half of which is "nonadministrative" faculty is to review faculty allocation to a discipline when enrollment drops below a specific level—10 percent below the three-year running average for the particular discipline at the particular campus. Enrollment declines are clearly related to the historical context of a discipline and a campus. The committee is required to advise the campus executive whether "special circumstances" warrant permitting further decline and resultant "overstaffing" and, if so, how a compensating increase in enrollment is to be achieved elsewhere on the campus. Stressing the distinction between programmatic change and enrollment decline, the task force Report proposes that the 10 percent "criteria shall not apply where reduced student-faculty ratios are the direct consequence of program changes." While the report may not represent the final word on layoffs in the California State University and Colleges, it clearly attempts to resolve issues that may have to be dealt with eventually by all systems. As in the Universities of North Carolina and Texas, an attempt is being made to anticipate, if not avoid, crisis.

In the Universities of California and Missouri, enrollment declines have occurred at individual campuses. In both, system-wide strategies have successfully avoided layoff of tenured but not of junior rank faculty. Both universities are also delaying the development of special procedures, in the belief that layoffs can be similarly avoided in the future.

In the University of Missouri, enrollment decline at the specialized Rolla campus in the early 1970s resulted in substantial overstaffing in some areas. In geology, for example, 11 faculty members had an average of only five students in each course, and approximately one dozen nontenured staff were terminated. Tenured faculty were not laid off; some were absorbed by an AID project, some were given research leaves or assigned to campus or systemwide research projects, and others were absorbed into the university extension program. (The university also operates a clearinghouse to advise other campuses of the availability of surplus faculty, but this is not considered of significant help in placement.) It is anticipated that enrollment will increase at Rolla, and that normal attrition will reduce faculty size to an acceptable level by the time faculty return from leave or foreign assignment. The ability of the University of Missouri to shift funds from campus positions to systemwide activities has been critical to this strategy.

Enrollment decline at the Riverside campus of the University of California resulted in more formal systemwide procedures than those in the University of Missouri. Between 1972 and 1975, 52 permanent positions—approximately one-sixth of the budgeted faculty—were lost at the Riverside campus. These are in the process of being absorbed through attrition with help from central administration in replacing permanently assigned faculty positions with temporary positions from a newly-created systemwide pool and in creating special procedures for permanent and temporary transfers to other campuses. Here, however, as at Rolla, the priority given to tenured faculty for retention has led to staffing imbalance in disciplines within the campus.

The use of a systemwide pool to alleviate temporary overstaffing and to allow time for actual and budgeted student-faculty ratios to converge through attrition appears unique to the University of California. California State University and Colleges, for example, retains 25 positions centrally to meet increases in student demand for specific programs, but state budget control language precludes using this pool to ease problems of enrollment decline.

The University of California also hopes that faculty layoffs at a specific campus can be avoided by intercampus transfers. Special procedures for such transfers were sent to campus executives with a clear statement that their use should be encouraged (University of California, 1974c): "I request you to take note of the fact that by appropriate use of intercampus transfers the consequences of a faculty cutback on a campus can be greatly ameliorated, faculty morale can be sustained and, I hope, the most serious personal hardships to faculty members can be avoided. Although an individual's right to appointment is confined to the campus of appointment, the size of the university and the diversity of opportunities within it may very likely make it unnecessary for the university to lose the services of a valued faculty member as a result of declining enrollments, financial exigency, or change in academic program."

In the University of California, as in the University of Missouri, substantial freedom from state control of campus student-faculty ratios is essential to orderly adjustment of faculty numbers to declining enrollment. Intercampus transfers are also clearly more feasible in systems with relatively equal tenure and salary regulations and with campuses having relatively equal program emphases than in systems with more heterogeneous campuses. Movement of faculty among campuses will not be the only solution to retrenchment in any system, however. Despite obvious practical advantages, mobility within multicampus systems will be highly restricted by overall resource constraints and by the campus-based nature of faculty appointments and interests.

Of the nine multicampus systems, only the University of Wisconsin was required to lay off tenured faculty as a result of recent enrollment declines. Its experience comprehends both the development of layoff procedures found at California State University and the preventive strategies undertaken at the Universities of Missouri and California. The University of Wisconsin experience is unique, however, in that there was neither time to prepare for nor flexibility to prevent the dislocation of faculty.

The federal court which heard the subsequent complaint of the aggrieved personnel succinctly stated the major causes of the crisis (*Johnson v. Regents,* 1974, p. 2): "The 1973-75 university system biennial budget approved by state government confronted units of the system with serious budget contraction. The principal ingredients of this problem were: (a) a flat requirement that there be a 2.5 percent reduction in the base budget of the system for 1973 1974, and another 2.5 percent reduction for 1974-1975; and (b) reduced enrollments on several campuses of the University of Wisconsin which, under state law, required a further reduction in funds available to those campuses."

As noted in the opinion, state law requires that campus budgets be reduced as enrollment declines. Although the university enjoys substantial budgetary flexibility, this requirement, combined with mandated "productivity savings" (a base budget reduction), made it impossible to shift sufficient resources to avoid layoffs, as in the Universities of California and Missouri. As the chief budget officer of another system noted, "flexibility doesn't mean a thing if you don't have anything to flex."

In early 1973, university administrators successfully sought a minimum amount of running room by obtaining a one time transitional appropriation to allow required one-year notices to tenured faculty. Special funding was necessary because of the state requirement that the university begin to repay funds in installments to the state as soon as fall enrollment is determined to be less than projected in the budget.

Initial decisions on procedures and specific layoffs were the responsibility of each campus executive under broad guidelines from central administration. Central administration then issued detailed guidelines for reconsideration procedures. These guidelines required that affected faculty members be given a written explanation for the layoff and notice that they were entitled to a hearing by a faculty committee on the sufficiency of the evidence supporting the layoff and whether or not the campus executive adhered to procedures for "determination of fiscal and programmatic needs of the university" (that is, established statutory budgetary formulas and administrative procedures derived from them). Some faculty members sought an injunction to prevent layoff, claiming that procedures violated the due process clause of the federal constitution.

In June 1974, the federal district court held that the university procedures were valid. The ruling stated that the initial layoff determination was a question of state and university policy and not governed by the federal constitution. The court also held, however, that a faculty member has a constitutional right to show (both within the institution and thereafter in court) that the dismissal was for a constitutionally impermissible reason (for example, violation of the right to free speech) or that the basis for the decision was wholly arbitrary. The court concluded that affected faculty members in Wisconsin had received this opportunity, noting that university procedures encompassed all elements of what the court termed "minimal procedures" (*Johnson v. Regents*, 1974, p. 21):

> I have concluded that these minimal procedures include: furnishing each plaintiff with a reasonably adequate written statement of the basis for the initial decision to lay off; furnishing each plaintiff with a reasonably adequate description of the manner in which the initial decision had been arrived at; making a reasonably adequate disclosure to each plaintiff of the information and data upon which the decisionmakers had relied; and providing each plaintiff the opportunity to respond.

Society should expect more of education leaders than that they avoid violating the constitutional rights of their faculty. The University of Wisconsin clearly went beyond the minimal procedures set by the court. One senior system administrator stated that the central administration tried "to make this as humane as possible when it's fundamentally an inhumane kind of process." Of the original group of 88 designated for layoff, only four actually were unemployed the following fall (without a job either within the university system or elsewhere), and these were either unwilling or unable to consider work at other campuses in the system.

Institutionally, central administration recognized early that the AAUP financial exigency guidelines required amplification to be made operational. Specificity was obtained by defining *exigency* as applicable either to an entire campus or to a subunit within a campus. In 1974, only provisions relating to a campus were invoked. Secondly, central administration determined that the decision that financial exigency existed was so critical that it should be made by the governing board. The administration further concluded that, if the governing board was to review dislocation of specific faculty members, such review should be limited to facts and procedures applicable to that particular person, and that broader and impersonal issues raised by fiscal and programmatic needs of a particular campus or the system should be resolved in advance.

With respect to aiding individual faculty members, current Wisconsin procedures allow campuses to offer displaced faculty members four types of designation. The first, reassignment status, allows for retraining or reassignment, either at the campus or within the system, but can be offered only if the campus can ensure funding for two years. The second, reassignment-layoff status, likewise allows for reassignment, but guarantees funding only during the one-year notice period. The third, relocation leave, releases the faculty member from his current assignment to seek relocation or retraining outside the system, and must be accompanied by a resignation effective upon the termination of the one-year notice period. The fourth designation, layoff status, is the required choice if a faculty member does not or cannot elect the other designations.

In addition, a systemwide staff member has full-time responsibility for assisting dislocated faculty in finding other positions. In the current academic marketplace, the task is not easy. If faculty grievances do not create academic positions where there are none, neither do administrative good intentions. Perhaps, however, the reward of aggrieved faculty is simply a day in court, and the reward of the administration is having a faculty member in layoff status state, as one did in the University of Wisconsin, "I really commend central administration for its efforts in trying to relocate us . . . they've done considerably more than they're obligated to do."

Related Issues

Financial exigency and overall enrollment declines are but the gross characteristics of retrenchment. Other equally pressing problems confront the multicampus system: what to do about faculty facing displacement through curricular change; whether tenure should be campus-based or systemwide; and the rights of tenured faculty as opposed to those without it.

Faculty specialization. Specific discipline specializations of faculty enter into discussion almost always in the context of the impact of past curricular decisions. Primary examples are the abolition of foreign language and history requirements for a baccalaureate degree. Based on apparently sound educational reasons in the 1960s, the decisions have resulted in more tenured faculty than many departmental enrollments can currently justify, at least on a comparative basis within the institution.

Although recognizing that such curricular changes create campus problems, administrators at the multicampus level show little interest in becoming actively involved. From a conference on the foreign language situation at State University of New York, a staff recommendation—as yet uncertain of implementation—did emerge that all students studying abroad should be required to have a basic knowledge of the particular language of the country in which they were to study. In other multicampus systems, similar conferences address similar problems. While these are often under multicampus aegis, systemwide activity is not much in evidence. For example, the question of whether the Davis campus of the University of California should or should not restore the foreign language requirement was not viewed as a matter for systemwide consideration.

Instead, in multicampus systems, decisions concerning academic program content have traditionally been deemed faculty matters or questions of campus concern. However, close interrelationships emerging in several systems between academic planning, program review, and budgeting may extend to considerations of faculty manpower planning, as evidenced in the proposed coordination of program review and faculty personnel planning in the California State University and Colleges

(1974b): "Academic program reviews should be conducted periodically and changes made, as necessary, to assure viable, responsible, and balanced curricula. Consideration should be given to faculty staffing requirements and to the need for renewal of faculty to assure optimal faculty utilization and maximal program effectiveness." In turn, campuses will be made more aware of the fact that seemingly innocent curricular judgments may have substantial resource implications and serious consequences for academic personnel.

Systemwide versus campus-based tenure. In 1970, the issue of system- versus campus-based tenure was not given explicit attention because, as we noted in our earlier study, dismissal of tenured faculty rarely occurred. At present, most multicampus systems—as well as distinguished outsiders—have given the matter much attention. Nevertheless, the issue remains unresolved. Two prestigious groups have reviewed the question and arrived at diametrically opposite conclusions. The Carnegie Commission on Higher Education (1972) suggested that "in multicampus institutions, employment contracts and tenure should be on a multicampus rather than on a particular campus basis. As overall growth declines, the rates of growth of different campuses may well continue to vary considerably. Thus one of the ways of retaining flexibility in the use of faculty in multicampus institutions may well be through shifting faculty members from campuses with stationary or declining enrollments to campuses with similar functions but with rising enrollments. However, we believe that such shifts should occur on a voluntary basis if at all possible."

A contrary conclusion is reached by the Commission on Academic Tenure in Higher Education (1973, p. 31) in a study sponsored by the Association of American Colleges and the American Association of University Professors: "The Commission believes that academic tenure must rest upon a judgment of competence for permanent service in a particular institutional setting and that this judgment must be made by the faculty in relation to the institution's own program and aspirations; therefore, where 'system' operations prevail, tenure should be held in the institution and not in the system as a whole." Thus, while the Commission recognizes that transfer of faculty among campuses might be desirable, its recommendations stress protection of the faculty member's campus-based tenure and the right of the individual campus to adhere to its own standards in the recruitment of faculty.

The same uncertainty is found in the nine multicampus systems under study. In general, unless a decision has been forced upon them, multicampus administrators have attempted to avoid the issue. The reason is obvious: campus-based tenure runs counter to the concept of a single university which most systems espouse. But systemwide tenure poses so many practical problems as to appear unrealistic. University counsel in Texas and California have given opinions that tenure is based at individual campuses. At the University of Texas, the opinion is consistent with other administrative procedures and confirms prior understanding. Underscoring campus prerogative, traditional tenure rules have been replaced by seven-year contracts at two Texas campuses. The University of California is perhaps more representative of prevailing uncertainty, however. Prior to the counsel's opinion, many believed that tenure was systemwide, although procedures did not explicitly so provide. Since that opinion, the central administration has operated in a manner consistent with campus-based tenure, but procedures are still silent. Sentiment remains divided both among faculty and among administrators; some of the latter carefully note that counsel's opinion is not actually university policy, and that circumstances have not yet required that such policy be formally promulgated. A definite tendency is evident, however, in the previously quoted presidential memorandum concerning intercampus transfers: "An individual's right to appointment is confined to the campus of appointment."

Administrators at several multicampus institutions and their attorneys have the question under consideration (and probably hope it will remain so until a case actually requires decision). In the State and City Universities of New York, collective bargaining and union suggestions that tenure is (or should be) a negotiable issue adds to the uncertainty. In the

City University, while tenure is generally recognized as campus-based, regulations require that when an individual transfers from one senior college to another, "years of continuous service at the first senior college are to be counted in computing the years of continuous service toward tenure at the second senior college" (City University of New York, 1974c).

In contrast, at both California State University and Colleges and the University of North Carolina campus-based tenure is a matter of express policy. For example, the code of the University of North Carolina (1973, p. 22) states that "in all instances, the tenure conferred on a faculty member is held with reference to employment by a constituent institution, rather than employment by the University of North Carolina." However, in California, the report of the powerful joint legislative conference committee on the 1974-75 budget states (State of California, 1974c):

> The California State University and Colleges [should] take all steps necessary to insure that faculty are not dismissed due to downturns in enrollment on any campus, including but not limited to the following: (a) That CSUC utilize any anticipated salary savings or other funds from positions which are not filled to provide for decreased student-faculty ratios in order to avoid the possibility of layoffs. (b) That CSUC provide, where qualifications are similar, that open academic positions on one campus be filled first by academic employees who are not to be reemployed on another campus because of downturns in enrollment on that campus.

The conference committee report, lacking the force of law, does not purport to change tenure regulations of the California State University system. In fact, the language makes no distinction between tenured and nontenured faculty. It clearly expresses legislative intent, however, that a major characteristic of system-wide tenure—transferability of faculty among institutions—should be implemented.

The University of Wisconsin is the only multicampus university having actual experience with systemwide tenure. Although its current policy specifies campus-based tenure, the 1973 layoff procedures discussed above were based on preexisting statutes. These were interpreted by the state attorney general as still in force and as specifying systemwide tenure in the former Wisconsin State University system. Only campuses of that previous system faced enrollment declines; guidelines issued by the system to those campuses required that open tenured positions be frozen, that displaced faculty members be considered for them, and that central staff monitor the process. Guidelines did not require transfer of faculty among campuses, but a campus having a vacant position was to give consideration to a displaced faculty member from another campus. The nature and extent of such consideration were not further specified.

Without attempting to oversimplify the complexities of the matter—or the possible intrusion of collective bargaining agreements—it is most likely that faculty tenure will be campus-based. The possibility of faculty relocation does not depend on systemwide tenure but on actual multicampus actions involving a particular faculty member, a particular campus, and a particular department. Multicampus systems must make every effort to ensure that fiscal and personnel regulations encourage intercampus transfers. It is doubtful, however, that an unwilling department will be forced to fill an increasingly scarce vacancy with a specific person based on membership in the system. In the area of faculty layoffs and retention, barring union or legislative intervention, the multicampus system provides only limited room for mandatory mobility among its campuses.

Priority in layoffs. In general, existing or proposed layoff procedures treat faculty members in three categories: tenured faculty; faculty who are full-time and on the tenure track; and part-time faculty. The priority of tenured faculty for retention is but one of a multitude of issues which arise in development of layoff procedures. These are not specific to the multicampus context, but unquestionably require systemwide attention and—

probably—uniformity. For example, in procedures adopted by the University of Wisconsin and proposed by the California State University and Colleges, program considerations take precedence over tenure. The task force report of the latter comments (California State University and Colleges, 1974d):

> Representatives of at least one faculty membership organization have recommended the termination of all nontenured faculty before any tenured faculty member is terminated. If this recommendation is meant to apply to disciplines, we believe that Title 5 provisions satisfy its intent. If it is meant to apply to institutions as a whole, we cannot endorse it, since that would entail what has been called an "attempt to rationalize a patchwork curriculum around existing tenured faculty."

Another such issue is seniority. If program considerations are satisfied, procedures generally require layoff to be in inverse order of seniority, but questions arise of whether seniority should be determined within professorial ranks or across ranks, and whether it should be determined by service in a department or at a campus. The California State University and Colleges task force report proposes that the determination of programs to be cut be discipline-based but the decision of whom to lay off within the program be determined by total length of service at the campus, regardless of how long the individual has been in the program. The administrative and personal complexities of this—or any other—proposed solution are obvious. Additional problems arise when the services of probationary faculty are no longer needed because of enrollment declines. Yet service towards tenure is valuable to the individual. Should the faculty member be laid off (with reemployment rights) or terminated? We can offer little advice on these issues other than that they must be resolved in detail within the context of state law and the regulations of each system. However, in keeping with both the procedures of the University of Wisconsin and the recommendations of the Commission on Tenure, we suggest the greatest flexibility and discretion possible should be left to faculty and administrators at campuses.

Inflation and Salaries

Substantial inflation has had specific impact on all multicampus systems. However shortlived inflationary trends may prove to be, they have already accelerated changes in salary administration that would otherwise have been caused by more general financial stringency over the next decade.

The first change is increased faculty pressure for across-the-board salary increases rather than discretionary increases based on merit. The University of Missouri affords the most striking example. Subject to systemwide review of salaries over $18,000, campus executives have had almost unlimited discretion in fixing individual faculty compensation. In 1974, for the first time in memory, the budget required that 4 percent of the 6 percent incremental increase be mandatory and across-the-board for cost of living, leaving the remaining 2 percent discretionary. Similarly, the University of North Carolina has received funds for salary increases since 1950 in the form of a lump sum for merit increases; in 1974, however, the faculty senate unanimously favored across-the-board allocation.

Pressure for across-the-board salary increases takes a different form in the State University of New York, where salaries are fixed through negotiations between the faculty bargaining unit and the governor's office. The current negotiated increase of 7 percent has been divided into 6 percent across-the-board and 1 percent merit. The bargaining unit urges, however, that collective bargaining negotiations in the future be limited to the across-the-board increment only. Central administration should, it is contended, make a separate case for merit increases in the course of regular budget negotiations. Cost of living is of interest to the union, merit is not.

Specifically related to the multicampus context, a second and related change may be seen in pressures in several systems for greater uniformity of salaries across campuses. Generally, as in the Universities of North Carolina, Texas, and Wisconsin, salary differentials are maintained among different types of campuses. In North Carolina, faculty resolutions have proposed equalization of salaries by rank across all of the widely differing campuses of that system. In Wisconsin, there is similar pressure from campuses of the former Wisconsin State University system to level upward.

Arguments for salary parity among campuses and for across-the-board salary increases without regard to merit are not persuasive. Assurance that fair and equitable compensation be paid to faculty should not entail complete elimination of salary flexibility. Diverse faculty talents command diverse compensation.

One thing does appear clear, however: multicampus systems will be required to give greater attention to salary administration at both system and campus levels in the future. Our earlier study (1971, p. 289) expressed concern over the lack of systemwide interest in salary administration: "Within most systems, the relative authority over salaries on the part of the department chairman, the college dean, and the campus executive varies from campus to campus, as does the extent of faculty involvement. Absence of uniformity is not surprising, but we found the lack of universitywide knowledge about salary practices among the campuses to be unwarranted and perhaps unwise. Most multicampus universities have established fairly uniform procedures to ensure that appointments and promotions are carried out with wisdom and equity, but the same cannot be said with respect to salary administration. The establishment of universitywide criteria and procedural standards is worthy of far more attention." Our concern continues.

The question of the exact form such attention should take must be left unanswered. Traditionally, faculty salaries are related to the highest degree offered by the campus, with research-oriented institutions commanding higher levels of compensation, particularly at the most senior ranks. A senior administrator at the University of North Carolina is not sure that this "really makes sense, even though it is still the rule in the marketplace." Explicit rules which recognize the marketplace yet reward dimensions of quality previously neglected will not be easy to devise—particularly in an era of scarce resources.

Tenure Impaction

The policy and procedural problems raised by reducing the size
of faculty are considered secondary in the State University of
New York to what one administrator described as "the inexorable march of younger faculty towards tenure." The method of
meeting tenure impaction in the State University is typical of
that in other multicampus systems. The system chief executive
is urging campus staff to review tenure procedures and faculty
distribution by age and tenure. Systemwide staff will monitor
campus reviews. In the State University, as in the University of
North Carolina, some campus executives would prefer that
quotas on the number of tenured faculty be set for campuses by
central administration. But systemwide quotas are universally
rejected as a limitation on multicampus flexibility. More importantly, such quotas would limit the flexibility of campuses,
where the essential qualifications for tenure should be determined and where program decisions are best made.

General guidelines at the system level must, however, be
translated into operational guides for campuses. Variations
among campuses approach their numbers, and our review of
campus guidelines can only briefly summarize a few of these. At
the University of Missouri, new tenure appointment procedures
at the campus level will, it is believed, limit such appointments.
At the Austin campus of the University of Texas, on the other
hand, deans have been asked to maintain existing proportions of
tenured to nontenured faculty within their schools. A similar
approach is found on at least two of the campuses of California
State University and Colleges.

At the Berkeley campus of the University of California, a
computer model projects estimated promotions available for
entry level appointments, promotions to tenure from within the
campus, and a small number of tenure appointments from outside the campus. On the other hand, the Santa Cruz campus,
faced with a relatively young faculty and little attrition through
retirement, is considering the appointment of older tenured faculty to provide a more balanced age distribution.

Campus plans will differ with the size, age, and capacity of
the campus to make internal adjustments. Whatever form plans

may take, multicampus systems must insist that campuses look to the future so that changing programmatic needs can be met by a faculty that is not unduly impacted by tenure.

Quotas and more intensive review may not prove sufficient, however, and other strategies are under consideration. For example, retirement plans such as those at the Universities of California and Wisconsin which permit early retirement to be complemented by part-time teaching, thus opening up positions for new appointees, are clearly a way to meet specific departmental problems. Such part-time appointment might be at a second campus within the system. However, the possibility of widespread implementation of such procedures is not promising, both because of high initial funding required and legislative and governing board attitudes. Indeed, in the State University of New York, the constitutionality of giving retirement pay to a working faculty member has been questioned.

The most liberal retirement plan among the nine systems—and possibly in the country—is that of the City University of New York, where retirement is allowed at age 50 after 20 years of service. The utility of such a plan for easing the impact of tenure has been questioned, however, on the basis that "the faculty you want to keep are the ones most likely to leave." And in all states, the issue is clouded by inflation: Faculty do not wish to retire early unless a cost-of-living factor is built into postretirement benefits. Here, as in so many other instances, inflation limits the ability of the multicampus system to respond creatively to the demands of a period of limited growth.

7

Strategies for Students: Admissions and Transfers

The defining characteristic of the unsteady state is the reduced rate of enrollment growth. Greater emphasis on academic plans and program review, faculty overstaffing and discontent, the troubled academic marketplace—all are basically derived from enrollment declines on some campuses and reduced expectations on others. In this environment, admissions and transfer policies within the multicampus system assume a new importance. But students, in voting with their feet among campuses and programs, are scarcely conscious of their impact upon systemwide concerns and priorities. Despite all that universities can do, student attendance remains a highly voluntary act.

Admissions and Transfers

In 1971, we reported (p. 456): "An evaluation of the multicampus university in terms of the admission and transfer of undergraduate students is clearly premature. For many reasons, external and internal, few of the systems have been forced to act like systems." Changing numbers of students and changing motivations have made many of the earlier issues moot, but systemwide admissions policies remain important, indeed crucial, as the enrollment plateau which has been a recent feature of higher education flattens even more. Demographic shifts, termination of the draft, reduction in the demand for school teachers, changes in the economy, and the changing life style of young adults are all contributing factors. But, in addition, each state and each system has its own set of problems. For example, the University of Wisconsin faced systemwide enrollment reductions in 1972-73, while the University of Texas was embarking on the establishment of three new campuses and appeared unperturbed by national projections of enrollment stabilization, if not downturns. But within each system, too, there are special —indeed contradictory—developments among the campuses. Even in Wisconsin, some campuses continue to grow, while in Texas, the El Paso campus saw its enrollment decline substantially in 1972. In the spring of 1974, the Urbana campus had already closed admissions to almost all programs, but at Chicago Circle previous deadlines were being extended in hopes that the campus would meet its target. Berkeley is bursting, but Riverside is in trouble. Even within the geographical confines of New York City, far more top-ranked students want to go to Queens than it can handle, while City College fights to attract them. Each state and each system has its unique pattern of enrollment distribution or maldistribution. Within the campus, a similar pattern is often revealed. Humanities enrollments are down, professional school enrollments are up; and systemwide overview of these internal adjustments is on the agenda of every central administration.

Confronted with a capital investment in physical plant and a human investment in tenured faculty, multicampus systems have reacted to enrollment problems in a variety of ways. Five areas in which changes can be made are discussed here: admissions policies, redirection of applicants to other campuses in the system, fees, coordination and articulation with community colleges, and transfer of students within system. Some related questions—the administration of financial aids, educational opportunity programs, quotas on nonresident admission to professional schools—are not considered; although important issues for every multicampus system, they are complicated by but not directly related to overall enrollment trends. Issues of graduate education, in contrast, are enrollment problems. For many campuses, the decline in graduate students, particularly at the doctoral level, is creating serious program imbalances. The universitywide doctorate, discussed previously, is an example of the response of one system. The changing pattern of graduate enrollments is not, however, basically an admissions problem, but one composed of student demand, perceived program quality, and the relationship between credentials and the marketplace. It is not discussed here.

Freshman Admissions Policies

At the time of our 1971 study, uniform and selective admissions standards were to be found only in California, where each of the two systems employed a universitywide policy, binding on all campuses within each system. By 1975, both the University of Missouri and the City University of New York had adopted uniform qualifications, applicable to freshman applicants to all campuses. In neither case, however, was the new policy a result of stabilizing or declining enrollments. The uniform Missouri policy replaced a high school class rank with a combined class rank and test score criterion, modestly increasing selectivity in the process. In marked distinction, the uniform standard of City University is an essential part of the open-admissions program (discussed below).

In the other five systems, in contrast, the basic responsibility for admissions standards continues to rest at the campus level, and expectations of increasing uniformity in standards have not materialized. The issue is best typified in the newly merged university systems of North Carolina and Wisconsin. Here, the heterogeneity of student clientele among the campuses has made it impractical, if not impossible, to standardize admissions requirements. As in the Universities of Illinois and Texas and the State University of New York, there are considerable intercampus variations in acceptable test scores and high school averages. Thus, of the University of Wisconsin four-year campuses, three draw from the upper 50 percent of high school graduates, nine from the upper 75 percent, while two do not utilize high school standing at all. In North Carolina, some campuses use test scores as a basis for an admission decision, while others do not.

In 1970, a principal concern with freshman admissions was that a specific campus would unilaterally raise its requirements as it neared capacity and students would be denied admission without adequate attention to where else they might go. This question has not disappeared, but it is now program-specific. Within the California State University and Colleges, for example, campuses offering impacted programs (those in which applications far exceed openings) are required to utilize supplemental admissions criteria which must have universitywide approval. In 1974-75, 12 programs were so identified, including such popular fields as nursing, architecture, and oceanography. (At California Polytechnic University, San Luis Obispo, for example, more than 1,200 persons applied for the 290 openings in architecture in 1974). In other systems, such decisions can be made by the campus without systemwide approval, and admissions requirements are frequently being tailored to program capacity.

The primary issue now, however, is quite the reverse: Systemwide administrators are concerned that campuses will lower freshman admissions standards in an attempt to recruit students, forestall enrollment declines, and avoid budget cuts and faculty layoffs. The problem is not yet a serious one, perhaps, but in almost every university one or more campuses have felt the pressure to relax requirements. In the 1974 questionnaire survey by the Center for Research and Development in Higher Education, University of California, Berkeley, 41 percent of 279 public senior college and university presidents responding reported that to increase enrollments undergraduate admissions standards had been modified "extensively" (8 percent) or "some" (33 percent) between 1968 and 1974. Six percent predicted that by 1980 such standards would be modified "extensively," another 37 percent said "some" (Glenny and others, 1975).

Universally, central administrators are under pressure to increase their cognizance of the problem. The issue is posed in a report of the State University of New York central administration: "Major changes in admissions policies of any campus or group of campuses are likely to have a significant ripple effect throughout the system. For instance, if the senior colleges suddenly open their admissions in order to meet enrollment projections, they may take students who would otherwise have enrolled in a community college. This may press the community college, whose budget is so closely geared to enrollment. It may also press the senior colleges, after a lag of two years, in meeting their projections of transfer students from the community colleges" (State University of New York, 1973, p. V-9). In New York State, the scramble by more than one senior college for freshman applicants brought complaints from neighboring community colleges that their "turf" was being invaded. The problem is not limited to relationships with community colleges however. A reduction of scholastic requirements for admission without equal attention to remedial work, for which few campuses are well prepared, is an automatic assurance of an increase in attrition. Indeed, already tentative evidence from at least one system indicates that retention has declined as campuses have dipped lower into the applicant pool. The potential budgetary consequences, not to mention the human costs, are substantial. Continued campus authority over admissions requirements may continue to be the general rule, but it will have to be accompanied by systemwide monitoring and—in states with separate community colleges—coordinating agency surveillance as well.

Redirection

As suggested, the plateauing of admissions is felt differently by each campus, even within the same system. Berkeley and UCLA reached their official ceilings some years ago, and neither appears to be in immediate danger of falling below those targeted figures. Austin and Urbana are talking for the first time about a limitation on ultimate campus size, and their admissions policies have reflected this concern by becoming more restrictive. Other campuses, while not yet faced with a ceiling are—from year to year—attracting students up to budgeted capacity in terms of a desired student-faculty ratio.

In each system, however, other campuses are struggling to meet their enrollment targets and are eager to attract students denied admission to the popular campuses. Central administrative staff members are concerned about this problem, for to the extent that students can be distributed (or distribute themselves) evenly throughout the university, budgetary and staff pressures can be eased.

But students are not easily redirected. Administrative procedures notwithstanding, there can be no assurance that a student denied admission to Urbana will go to Chicago. (He is just as likely to go to Madison.) Nor will a Berkeley applicant easily be redirected to Riverside, or a Queens applicant to City College. The mobility of students within states and between them, between campuses and programs, is difficult to analyze and even more difficult to predict. Faced with this reality and without the earlier pressure to absorb growth, the nine systems vary in response from no activity at all, through admissions relocation assistance, to formal redirection programs.

Admissions relocation assistance is perhaps best exemplified by the Wisconsin Higher Education Location Program (HELP). Initiated in March 1973 as a pilot project, the program has now been given permanent status. It is both a toll-free, telephone clearinghouse (locally termed a hot line) for questions concerning the university system and a referral service for persons seeking information about a specific campus (which then contacts the caller). More than seven hundred calls were received by HELP during the four-month pilot period, and the central administration believes that the program has clearly proved its worth, particularly given the variations—and potential public confusion—in campus admissions requirements in the Wisconsin system. In addition, a recently adopted common admissions and financial aid application is used by all campuses.

However, further centralization in Wisconsin is deemed unnecessary because few students apply to more than one campus—about 15 percent of total applicants in 1974. Reduced demand, combined with the absence of campus ceilings on enrollment, has lessened pressures for systemwide activity, and virtually all students are now admitted to the campus of their first choice. But if the phase-down-phase-out plans reported in Chapter Two are implemented, interest in centralized procedures may be revived.

The same pattern is evident in the State University of New York, where—unlike Wisconsin—a centralized admissions procedure is in effect. Students may apply to several campuses (each of which has its own requirements), utilizing only a single application form and indicating to the central administration (but not to the campuses) their choice of campus. Students denied admission to their first-choice campuses may use the services of an admissions assistance center to locate campuses at which there are openings and for which they are qualified. In 1973-74, 750 persons made inquiries, but only 35 of them reapplied to a senior college campus suggested to them by the center. It is believed that most of the others enrolled in community colleges, but no tracking mechanism is presently available.

Although the University of Texas generally has campus-based admissions also, an important experiment in centralization is taking place there. Applications of medical and dental students are centrally processed, and a computerized analysis is sent to each school. However, the individual units both review the applications and interview the applicants separately, despite only marginal differences in student ratings. The costs in time and energy of the present system for both the faculty and the applicant are, of course, immense.

In the City University of New York the picture is dramatically different because of the guiding policies of the system: open admission of all high school graduates, ethnic integration, and quality education. Implementation of these goals thus necessitates complicated and centralized admissions policies and procedures. All New York City high school graduates are placed in rank order, based either on rank in their high school graduating class or on their high school average, whichever is higher. Students are then assigned to the campus of their choice on the basis of this rank order until the campus enrollment target (based on space and budget) is reached. Some 75 percent of students have been accommodated at their first-choice campuses under this system, including virtually all students with a high school average of 85 or over.

However, and the qualification is a critical one, each campus is also required to enroll its share of entering students not qualified on scholastic grounds but expressing a desire to attend the institution. In 1972-73, out of some 35,000 freshman applicants, 1,700 students with high school averages below 70 were admitted to senior colleges of their choice.

The dilemma confronting the City University in administering this admissions program is perhaps unique, but the results of attempts to resolve it apply in all systems which try to adjust enrollments among campuses: The best students are the least likely to accept redirection; refused entrance to their preferred campus, they may well enroll outside the university. Paradoxically, however, the same result occurs with some of the poorest students, whose motivation for higher education is often weak to start with; denied admission to their preferred campus, they often drop out entirely. Motivating both the highly qualified and the marginal student is a dual goal of the City University system. That the goals have contradictory elements is suggested by a memorandum to the City University trustees (City University of New York, 1974c):

> An allocation system which effectively bars almost all minority students from a particular college and thus establishes an all-white college in the city system is doomed intolerable. On the other hand, there is a pervasive feeling in some quarters that permitting students with lower academic averages to gain entrance to a particular college ahead of some students with higher averages is unjust and unfair. The university must establish policies which reconcile these two opposing points of view.

While the City University open-admissions program has as a basic element the redirection and assignment of poorly qualified students to the campuses of that system, the program of the University of California involves the redirection of highly qualified applicants who meet uniform and quite restrictive admissions standards but are not accepted by their first-choice campus. In 1974, two campuses were faced with qualified applicants in excess of capacity: Berkeley, because of its fixed enroll-

ment ceiling, and Davis, because of its budgeted target enrollment. (Berkeley was forced to redirect approximately 1,500
freshman applicants, Davis 1,000.)

Applicants to the University of California are given preference as to campus based on their high school grade point averages. However, the campuses also select students from the qualified pool on the basis of such criteria as financial hardship,
family location, academic programs, and the need on a large
residential campus to achieve a balance between men and
women.

The need for redirection will diminish within the university, it is anticipated, as the pool of applicants declines and as
the newer campuses expand and more program options become
available. This lessening of the need for redirection has largely
occurred already within a parallel program of the California
State University and Colleges, where applicants may choose an
alternate campus at the time of application. In 1974, only 812
students, less than 1 percent of the applicants during the initial
filing period, were redirected to a campus of second choice. In
contrast, in 1971 the comparable figure was 8,500, nearly 10
percent of total applicants.

Even at the peak of the redirection process, however, the
California experience was that a substantial portion of redi-
rectees did not register at the alternate campus. In 1971, for
example, only 40 percent of redirected undergraduate applicants within the University of California system did so. The
lesson for the multicampus system is clear. In a period of plateauing enrollments and excess capacity at campuses across the
nation, systemwide attempts to regulate the attendance of
highly mobile students—transferring them from campuses at
capacity to a campus crying for students—may well be futile.
The burden will be on the campus to attract students and not
on the system to redirect them.

Reducing Fees

In addition to lowering admissions standards and redirecting
students, another possible solution to enrollment problems is
reducing fees. In an attempt to attract students, the University
of Wisconsin reduced fees at two of its lower-division center

campuses from $250 per semester to $40, the average fee charged at adjacent vocational-technical institutions. Based on a survey of the affected students, the central administration concluded that "upwards of three hundred students attended the centers who may likely have not without the reduced fees" (University of Wisconsin, 1974a). Enrollments at the adjacent vocational schools increased as well. This seemingly modest experiment is, in fact, fraught with significant policy implications, which may prove critical in the years ahead. The issue of differential pricing policies for different kinds of postsecondary education has nevertheless been joined by the central administration in Wisconsin, the multicampus university hardest hit by lack of enrollment growth (University of Wisconsin, 1974c, p. 3):

> We have reached a point where access to public university institutions and programs is being negatively affected by spiraling costs to students . . . . The other major public postsecondary system [Vocational, Technical and Adult Education] (VTAE) operates with a state and local taxpayer subsidy that *positively encourages* citizen access to its programs through considerably lower fees. Rather than facing critical scrutiny for declining enrollments and overbuilding, this excellent VTAE system faces the happy challenges of burgeoning enrollments and capital expansion, while we face the difficult problem of dual-priced competition with its growing college-parallel program. . . .
>
> Simply stated, the smaller, high-cost campuses— centers and universities—cannot extricate themselves, nor be extricated by some miraculous act of a merged system, from a situation where a different "pricing" policy (due to a smaller percentage of public subsidy) works against their effective utilization.

Senior College-Community College Relationships

In all states, growing competition between the senior colleges and the two-year institutions for students, funds, programs, and public support may emerge as a key issue as students and funds diminish. Multicampus systems bear part of the responsibility for the creative containment of this competition. Differential fees and the possible impact upon two-year college enrollments of changes in senior college admissions requirements are but two problems in this area. Others remain.

The first issue can be quickly dealt with, although it may become critical and controversial: the division of programs between four- and two-year institutions. In Wisconsin, for example, some vocational-technical schools have increasingly offered college-preparatory work, previously the exclusive province of the senior institutions and the lower-division centers.

In North Carolina, an opposite concern is emerging—that the four-year campuses will be tempted to offer two-year paraprofessional programs generally considered to be the province of the community colleges. Indeed, some of the small senior colleges currently offer two-year vocational programs, and competition for students (and funds) is immediate. At the same time, North Carolina shares the Wisconsin concern over encroachment by two-year campuses into its bailiwick. In both states, responsibility for governance of senior and two-year institutions is divided. Merger of the four-year and university campuses has left for future consideration the distribution of programs vis-a-vis the two-year schools. The issue will not quickly or easily be resolved.

A second issue is acceptance of two-year college courses for baccalaureate-degree credit and articulation of specialized programs between the two-year and senior institutions. The situation in Missouri is described by some as "a constant battle" between each of the four campuses of the university and the community colleges, with the central administration attempting to negotiate agreements satisfactory to all parties. A truce appears imminent because the senior campuses have become interested in attracting qualified transfer students as enrollments decline. In North Carolina, the campuses establish their own transfer requirements, but community college graduates are virtually assured of acceptance at the campus of their choice —unless it is Chapel Hill. A similar pattern prevails in Texas. In the two New York systems, admission to one of the senior institutions is guaranteed to any student receiving an associate of arts degree, and almost every student has been accepted by the campus of first choice.

A formal agreement between the California State University and Colleges and the exceedingly strong community colleges in the state provides another pattern. In essence, the 19 State University campuses have agreed to accept the decision of each community college as to which of its courses are suitable for baccalaureate credit. A joint board has been established by the two segments to arbitrate disputes, but the burden of proof rests upon the State University to prove that a course or program should not receive full collegiate credit. Contrary to the expectations of many, a general tightening of requirements has resulted because of conscientious review by community college administrators. The University of California has not followed this procedure, but continues independently to certify all community college programs for which a transfer of credit is anticipated. The community colleges submit virtually no programs which are not certified, and the occasional disagreements are usually quickly and informally resolved.

In sum, an end to articulation disputes, long the bane of admissions officers, may be one of the beneficial results of current enrollment trends. Unnecessary requirements and barriers to transfer are falling under the pressure to attract students. Here, however, as with freshman admissions requirements, central administration monitoring will be required to ensure that appropriate standards are retained. It would be unfortunate if the end result of improved articulation was merely to increase the attrition rate at the upper-division level.

Intercampus Transfer

Just as with transfers from two-year colleges, reduced enrollment has led to a general lowering of barriers to transfer between campuses of the university. Most campuses are pleased to welcome students from sister institutions, although the sending campus may be equally reluctant to see them go. But the pressures that lead campuses to accept transfer students have not led to a significant increase in formally designed educational programs in which students move from one campus to another. Although several such plans are in prospect, experience is limited. In general, transfers within the system are based on individual student preference, rather than on coordinated multicampus programs.

The extent of intercampus transfer is not uniformly reported and is difficult to summarize. For 1973-74, the University of California reports that, out of a total undergraduate student body of some 80,000, more than 2,700 (3 percent) transferred from one campus of the university to another. In Missouri, a study of 1972-73 students indicates that 758 (2 percent) of the approximately 37,000 undergraduates transferred among the four campuses. In North Carolina, 1,235 (1 percent) of the approximately 90,000 undergraduates transferred from one campus to another in the fall term of 1973, while in the California State University and Colleges, 3,287 (less than 2 percent) of the approximately 210,000 students so transferred in the fall of 1972. These figures probably are the maximum. Most of the other systems report that the number of intercampus transfers is "minimal," and data are not centrally maintained as to their extent.

In the Universities of California and Missouri, the facilitation, if not the promotion, of intercampus transfer is a matter of universitywide policy. In California, for example, intercampus transfers among the relatively homogeneous student body of the university are given priority over community college graduates or transfers from campuses outside the university system. Missouri is attempting to develop a policy which will grant a student transferring within the system course credit for work taken at the first campus, even if the receiving campus does not offer a parallel course. Other systems are providing similar benefits. University of Illinois students may transfer to and from the Urbana and Chicago campuses with a lower grade average than is required for students transferring from outside the system. An undergraduate student transferring within the University of Texas system may be given a partial offset against the senior-year campus residence requirement.

Nevertheless, intercampus transfers are not an important

part of systemwide planning and probably will not be in the foreseeable future. Decisions by students, not by system administrators, will be the basic determinants of intercampus mobility. But a contradictory theme may develop. As suggested in our earlier discussions of academic planning, program review, and budgeting, difficult decisions must be made in the allocation of specific programs to specific campuses. The multiversity campus with something for everyone may continue in Austin or Berkeley, Madison or Urbana. But for most of the other campuses, choices must be made, and programs will be limited. In such an environment, students may increasingly wish to develop their individual programs not by picking a single campus but by utilizing the resources of two or more. Enrollment stabilization and fiscal stringency may make it easier both for the student to do so and for the multicampus system to develop systemwide opportunities for those students who could so benefit. In only a few places, however, have these opportunities so far been offered.

8

Multicampus Systems in the 1980s

In 1967, Gardner presented a criterion for assessing the effectiveness of a modern university in an unpredictable environment: "We do not need more change as such. We need more *intentional* change—specifically, the kinds of change in our institutions that will enable them to adapt to the radically altered circumstances in which they are now forced to function" (pp. 318-319). In 1971, we cited Gardner's prescription and went on to suggest that "the promotion of 'intentional change' through academic planning is one of the most frequently given reasons for the establishment and continued existence of the multicampus university" (p. 215).

What was desirable with universities still in the flush of rapid growth is now a necessity as higher education confronts the coming decade—a turbulent and dynamic unsteady state characterized by shrinking and shifting enrollments, new program thrusts, changing markets, an aging faculty, the prospect of collective bargaining, the increasing involvement of governors, legislators, and their staffs, and, above all, by limited resources.

The challenge which will confront the multicampus system in the next decade has been characterized by Kenneth E. Boulding as "the management of decline," and he suggests that we are ill-equipped to deal with it (Boulding, 1974): "very large adjustments will have to be made in our ways of thinking, in our habits and standards of decision-making, and perhaps even in our institutions. . . . In a growing institution mistakes are easily corrected; in a declining institution they are not. . . . Education is likely to be the first major segment of the economy to suffer a relative decline, and management of this decline may very well set the tone for the management of the general slowdown." Whether one talks of administering the unsteady state or the management of decline, it is evident that multicampus systems in the 1980s will be called upon to behave in new and different ways. As Boulding implies, lessons and experience of an era of growth may not be relevant in a period of static resources.

But new experience is being gained daily. It is the burden of preceding chapters that slowdowns and retrenchment—present or anticipated—have resulted in more intensive planning and program review, in new approaches to resource allocation, and in academic programs involving more than one campus. From this growing experience, we conclude that intentional change is taking place.

Our focus is on systemwide strategies directly involving central administration and on system activities designed to aid campuses in confronting the realities of the 1980s. In both cases, we repeat our admonition that these are new phenomena, to be measured in months rather than years. We would also reiterate that we have not reviewed many critical elements of the higher education scene, despite their obvious relevance to multicampus systems: for example, medical education, library management, the administration of computer centers, affirmative action. These are critical problems now. They will not lessen in the years ahead.

In short, the experience from which we draw is limited, and is changing even as we write. A sense of urgency is everywhere and decisions are demanded, but a note of caution, of tentativeness, of experimentation is essential. What then may we conclude about multicampus systems and the 1980s? While we cannot speak with authority about other kinds of multicampus systems—collegiate or community college—important lessons can be learned from the nine multicampus universities which we have examined here. Enrollment plateaus and budget constraints, academic planning and program review, student admissions and faculty retrenchment are universal concerns. The following comments, drawn from the experience of nine university systems but completely applicable to none, suggest the directions in which all multicampus systems must move in the coming decade.

Academic Planning

Perhaps the major change across the nine multicampus systems is the dramatically increased emphasis on academic plans and planning procedures. Five years ago such plans, when they existed, were largely compendia of campus aspirations—public relations statements rather than operational guidelines. Plans still present the public stance of the university, but now they also function as working documents that explore options and alternatives among campuses on the basis of realistic demographic and fiscal projections, and are subject to continuing analysis and revision. It is too early to know if such statements will help multicampus systems maintain effectiveness, but prospects are good.

Academic plans are now in the mainstream of governance and are the direct concern of system chief executives and senior administrators. Planning statements explicitly recognize that times are difficult and expected to be more so. While projections of enrollment and physical facilities must still reach ten or 15 years into the future, operational details of academic program planning rarely extend beyond the first five. Current reality has tempered earlier enthusiasm for long range—in retrospect, ivory tower—plans. General goals and missions remain an essential part of plans but are now supplemented by academic-program projections that are sufficiently specific to be operational. Frequent review of operational objectives—often coordinated with the annual or biennial budget cycle—is also required by the planning process.

Systemwide academic plans vary widely in content and specificity. Exceedingly specific plans are achieved at the cost of flexibility and perhaps unnecessary anticipation of hard decisions. On the other hand, more general plans may be suspect as lacking substance. Each system must determine the necessary balance between specificity and generality in terms of its own situation. None, however, can avoid a conscious search for it.

Academic Program Review

In quantity and quality, the growth of academic program review essential for successful implementation of plans matches the increased emphasis on planning. Five years ago the focus was limited to new programs, and important questions were whether a new program was appropriate for a particular campus and whether the campus was academically ready to undertake it. Both remain critical questions, but have been given added depth. The question of appropriateness has become very specific, based on examination of student opportunities, similar programs at other system campuses, and supporting programs at the requesting campus. The question of readiness continues to focus on availability of faculty, library, and other appropriate resources. Now, as in the past, the question of where additional resources will come from looms large, but the possible set of answers is very often narrowed to one: new programs must be funded by reallocation from existing ones. Indeed, the fiscal impact of program change is universally the third critical question posed to proponents of new programs.

Other aspects of new program review also reflect recent changes in most systems. Early warning notices or letters of intent are often required before full-scale proposals are submitted, and the stringency of formal review procedures often varies with the expected fiscal impact of the new program. Moreover, procedures previously limited to doctoral programs are being extended in many instances to master's and undergraduate programs as well. Central information systems now play a larger role, providing campuses with a wide range of comparable data about similar programs elsewhere in the system. Although conventional wisdom has it that such information systems lead to centralized decisions, experience thus far points instead to more informed campus ones.

Routine or structured review of existing academic programs is new to most systems and a major change over the past five years. Although initiated by the legislature or a coordinating agency in many instances, reviews of existing programs have rapidly become a permanent part of multicampus governance. As yet, however, firm procedural patterns have not developed. Reviews are initiated and performed directly under auspices of central administration when similar programs are reviewed across campuses. Such lateral reviews tend to be undertaken only as the need arises, for example, when a request for a new program triggers interest in existing ones. Other purposes include information needed for formal planning and, implicit in all such reviews, for more rational distribution of programs across campuses.

Reviews at the campus level may be undertaken at campus initiative, of course. The clearly emerging system role, however, is to require campus program reviews, either under systemwide guidelines or under campus guidelines which the system approves. Periodic review—usually at five-year intervals—is often required of all programs.

The rapid growth of existing program review is not without difficulties. Where the aim of review is primarily the improvement of programs at a single campus, it is in the nature of internal accreditation and raises few problems. Most often, however, reviews are undertaken to facilitate central administrative decisions on resource allocation—to determine which program to support at the expense of another. Evaluations to date have doubtless been useful but would increase in effectiveness if more were known about the evaluation process itself. Who should be the evaluators? Should they come from inside the system, outside the system, or both? How do costs of evaluation measure up to results? What is the relationship between systemwide evaluation procedures and those undertaken by an accrediting body or a statewide coordinating agency?

Each system is now answering these questions on an ad hoc basis as procedures are developed. Different systems and occasions require different answers. For example, a balance must be maintained between external and internal evaluators depending on the mission to be accomplished: external evaluators can strengthen quality control and credibility in review of specific programs, while internal evaluators can provide an intimate working knowledge of intercampus relationships. System-wide efforts should be coordinated with reviews by state agencies and accrediting bodies to minimize costs of review and to avoid unnecessary redundancy.

Such matters must be examined in each system and state to determine conditions under which different approaches are desirable, for the next decade will see a rapid increase in the review of existing programs. Increasingly critical academic decisions will be informed by the results of such evaluations. A continuing evaluation of the evaluations is a necessity.

Academic Budgeting

Operating budgets move academic program priorities from rhetoric to reality. Budgets were critical in times of growth, but are even more so today. In earlier years, continuing expansion meant flexibility, for the average cost of an additional student— a figure used to acquire funds—generally exceeded the actual marginal cost. Growth also meant self-correction, for enrollment increases in the following year caught up with errors in the budget period. Now, additional students are increasingly rare, and if enrollments decline, mechanical adherence to the same formulas could reduce funding below cost savings.

Although good reasons can be stated for changing the relationship, enrollment remains the critical factor in state funding: numbers of students and numbers of dollars are still related. Both system and state budgetary agencies use enrollment formulas and guidelines of varying complexity. Although formulas may be changing, there is no indication that they will disappear (nor, we should add, that they are being mechanically applied). States have recognized that time is needed to adjust to enrollment shifts. Budgetary procedures generally allow adjustments throughout the budget year and, in an instance in which they did not, one-time transitional funding was separately appropriated. Systems have retained the flexibility to shift appropriated funds among campuses and programs to meet shifting student demand (or lack of it).

We may expect—and hope—that budgetary procedures will continue to allow maximum systemwide flexibility consistent with accountability for public funds. The authority of the multicampus system must permit it to encourage one campus to fund and staff programs differently from other campuses in a system; the maintenance of such authority is a prime objective of systemwide administrators. State officials, whether in the executive office or the legislature, are often aware of this need but have other constituencies, other objectives, and other priorities. It is essential, therefore, that responsibility for meeting state fiscal objectives be imposed upon multicampus systems as systems. Economies, where they must be achieved, should generally be accomplished by reallocation within and by the system itself.

Although crisis exists in only a few systems, all are painfully aware of adjustments required to meet current economic inflation. Uncertainty of federal and extramural funds further reduces the necessary guarantee of fiscal flexibility required in times of resource constraint. Funds such as indirect cost reimbursement from grants and contracts are less available as a source of discretion, as they are diverted to activities previously supported by the state. Similarly, faculty collective bargaining may make inroads on fiscal flexibility as unallocated dollars are required to caulk the seams of negotiated contracts.

The analytic capacity of state executive and legislative budget agencies is increasing. Although potentially beneficial, the immediate impact is mixed, and there is a need to define more explicitly the boundary between legitimate state fiscal concerns and educational prerogatives of multicampus systems. In some instances, state probes seem unconstrained by an understanding of costs of response or the utility of such probes to senior state officials and budget officers. Staggered response deadlines, avoidance of duplicate inquiries, prior agreement on the precise reason for inquiry and the result desired, and costs and priority of requests should be among the minimal conditions of any state inquiry. Self-restraint on the part of governors, legislators, and their staffs is essential to avoid unnecessary and possibly harmful intervention into internal management of university academic affairs.

Similarly, procedures must be devised to separate educational policy from fiscal decisions wherever possible. The annual or biennial budget will remain the major vehicle for communicating state policy to higher education, but it should not become a catchall for policies which, however worthy, have only peripheral financial implications. As the margin for error in deciding critical fiscal questions narrows, the decision process should not be confused by other issues more appropriately resolved in other forums. For example, budget control language should not be used to mandate a particular organizational structure or staffing pattern within the multicampus system.

We do not suggest that educational policy decisions are never proper subjects for state consideration. A new medical school, a major shift in admissions qualifications, the closing of a campus are questions of state policy beyond the confines of the institution. But discussion and resolution of such issues should not be dominated by the specific thrust and inexorable force of the budget process.

Strategies for Program Development

In the past five years, systemwide academic activity has increased significantly in three related areas: nontraditional education, multicampus programs (including regional coordination), and innovative and experimental programs. Enrollment and resource constraints have been prime motivating factors for only one of these, multicampus programs. But all three have the potential to increase system effectiveness in a period of fiscal stringency and to enhance learning for the same (or a lower) cost.

Nontraditional education—off-campus, degree-credit programs for part-time students—has become an important activity in only three systems, although it is being discussed in others. However, it holds the promise of permitting low-cost experimentation with new programs and new students without major and permanent resource commitments. Specific student demands, the permanence of which cannot adequately be assessed, can be tested. In short, nontraditional education can serve a continuing research and development function for the system. Although the open education movement may have lost momentum, continuation of existing programs and experimentation with new ones should be encouraged and evaluation of both intensified.

Multicampus academic programs have grown substantially in recent years, and much of this activity is clearly attributable to the need to stretch increasingly limited resources across a wider front. Perhaps the most ambitious examples are the existing City University graduate center and the proposed Missouri systemwide doctoral degree. Both promise more effective resource allocation but also pose the problem of assigning faculty to inevitably limited advanced graduate programs. In New York, the development of a select critical mass of faculty at the graduate center must be balanced against aspirations of a larger number of faculty from several campuses. In Missouri, danger exists that campus-based program quality will be lost under pressures from other campuses for equal treatment or from costs in time and energy of joint programs separated, not by subway, but by freeway. A solution satisfactory to all parties is not in the offing, but lessons from these two systems will have relevance for higher education everywhere as attempts are made to allocate advanced graduate work.

Regional coordination—evidenced, for example, in Texas, Wisconsin, and the State University of New York—represents the most impressive recent effort in multicampus programs, an effort directly attributable to incentives to avoid unnecessary duplication among neighboring campuses. In all three instances, the role of central administration has been to stimulate development of regional arrangements rather than to manage them. Active system leadership, more stable funding, and a voice in the state capital give these regional experiments an added strength and credibility deriving from membership in the larger multicampus system. Regional arrangements offer a practical halfway house between campus autonomy and centralized program direction, providing another example of how resource constraints can lead, not to centralization, but to deliberate strategies of decentralization.

Multicampus programs, regionally organized or otherwise, do not necessarily save money but do give students and faculty program new options. From this perspective, they are cost-effective. Such programs should be encouraged by central administrative leadership and resources, and by reform of systemwide and campus procedures which unnecessarily inhibit student and faculty mobility and development of joint programs.

Innovative instructional programs—new approaches and experiments in undergraduate education—are a major item on the agenda of systems (as opposed to campuses) in only two or three of the multicampus universities. The action is with faculty and students at the campuses, and this is as it should be. There remains a role for central administration, however, in serving as a catalyst to stimulate innovative activity, to communicate experimental results throughout the entire system, to provide funding and—above all—to ensure effective evaluation. Gimmicks and fads in undergraduate education are all too easily and uncritically accepted. Central administration should either serve as an independent evaluator or monitor campus policies and procedures for sound evaluation.

Strategies for Faculty

The most obvious casualty of retrenchment is the faculty member who is laid off or fails to be reappointed because of enrollment cutbacks and resulting fiscal constraints. Less obvious but no less significant is the young Ph.D. who confronts an oversaturated job market and finds his professional career virtually terminated before it starts. For the institution, problems are more subtle. How can a "knowledge industry," as the modern university has been characterized, be made viable without continual introduction of new blood? How can a relatively static and aging faculty effectively deal with changing program emphases and new disciplinary demands? Experience of multicampus systems with such questions is limited, but consciousness is high that answers must be found if the institutions are to meet their responsibilities in the 1980s.

With specific reference to easing the personal trauma of retrenchment, the multicampus system has undoubted advantages. Campuses need adequate lead time to make program and personnel adjustments; time can be obtained by temporary transfers of positions from other campuses, by utilization of a systemwide pool of temporary positions, or by a combination of the two. The effectiveness of such strategies has been proven in the last two years. However, the flexibility of the multi-campus system is constrained externally by the need to maintain credibility with state officials concerned with imbalance in student-faculty ratios among campuses and internally by pressures among campuses for equity of treatment. Nevertheless, such flexibility is critical if multicampus systems are to operate as systems.

But even the greatest flexibility may not avoid layoffs. Indeed, deliberate program changes can require them. Preparation for possible retrenchment is a necessity. The experience in Wisconsin in which layoff of tenured faculty was required and in other systems considering layoff procedures—whether of tenured or nontenured faculty—indicates that procedures must carefully distinguish among at least three types of layoffs—layoffs required because of enrollment declines, those resulting from deliberate changes in program, and those which might result from base budget reductions (whether or not related to enrollment). As a matter of practice, governing boards should not become involved in specific personnel actions unless system appellate procedures so provide. However, trustees should generally be expected to make a finding, as in Wisconsin, concerning the existence of conditions requiring layoff. The importance, for example, of an acceptable definition of fiscal emergency and of procedures for dealing with such an emergency cannot be overestimated.

Decisions concerning specific faculty to be laid off are almost always campus matters. However, while some campus flexibility is permissible, policies and procedures governing these decisions must be generally uniform if systemwide equity is to be maintained and if the system is to be able to withstand legal challenge. In developing such policies, the ambiguity in existing AAUP guidelines will have to be resolved. A specific issue is the potential conflict between the policy calling for preferential treatment for a tenured faculty member in a layoff situation and the accompanying provision that "judgments determining where within the overall academic program termination of appointments may occur involve considerations of educational policy" (American Association of University Professors, 1974). Conflicts between seniority and program balance must be resolved, and the outcome must certainly avoid development of a curriculum dominated by tenure considerations. Multicampus administrators, one step removed from the personal pressures of the moment, must monitor campus decisions closely in the interest of program balance. As one system executive put it: "No problem is more worrisome than the thought that we might not be able to maintain program integrity in the face of the grave personnel pressures inevitably involved in the sensitive thicket of tenure layoff."

In all layoff cases, tenure or not, central administration staff can play a significant role in developing policies and programs in such areas as intercampus transfers, retraining, and relocation. The sensitive handling of such matters in Wisconsin stands as a model of action. In general, system policies should require that all campuses give good faith consideration to a person facing layoff from another campus within the system. Existing barriers to intercampus transfer should be eliminated and procedures developed to facilitate it. We believe, however, that tenure should be campus-based, not systemwide. Regardless of the apparent theoretical merits of systemwide tenure as a concept, we do not think mandatory mobility can be practically implemented.

Quite apart from issues of retrenchment and layoff, many institutions recruited largely from a narrow age group in the 1960s and now confront the dilemma of a relatively static and aging faculty. As a result, much greater attention must be given to the problem of faculty renewal. Although this is essentially an issue for departmental and campus resolution, central administration of multicampus systems should take the lead by reviewing the staffing pattern on each campus and establishing policies and guidelines where more will be required in many institutions.

We concur with the opinion of virtually all systemwide

administrators that tenure quotas should not be set either at the system or the campus level. However, we distinguish between quotas which state that only a fixed proportion of faculty can be advanced to tenure (no such plan exists in any of the nine university campuses) and personnel plans which divide faculty positions into two groups, tenure-track and temporary. The creation of a campus pool of temporary positions, from which a position can be assigned to a department facing a renewal problem, is one existing strategy which should be carefully considered by all systems as a matter of policy.

Retirement plans which include early retirement options or allow part-time work are useful, though often costly, in faculty personnel planning and in reducing layoff of younger faculty. Although not a problem peculiar to the multicampus structure, system administrations—by virtue of their size and expertise—can do much to undertake necessary studies and implement steps to initiate such optional approaches.

The variety of salary procedures and authority among campuses in most systems is as prevalent today as when we reported in 1971. In times of increasing concern over compensation brought about by collective bargaining, inflation, and budgetary cutbacks, it is doubtful that these unintentional and unmonitored practices will, or should, be allowed to continue. The end result need not be in the direction of centralization, but in systemwide insistence that campuses have effective policies and practices which can stand public scrutiny.

Strategies for Students

Compared to other matters included in this study—budgeting, academic planning, program review—systemwide activity in student affairs, here limited to admissions and transfers, remains relatively untouched by curtailment of growth in the mid-1970s. Problems of enrollment plateaus and declines are largely campus- and program-specific, and there appears little that multicampus systems, as systems, can do about these internal imbalances. Students, unlike budgets, are not readily transferable from one campus to another, and—as with the faculty—forced mobility is simply not an effective strategy.

Nevertheless, important systemwide issues and decisions demand attention. In 1971 these centered around provision of places for a burgeoning student body. Today, issues focus on a shrinking applicant pool and the ripple effect of unilateral campus action on the system as a whole.

Declining enrollments can create pressures on campuses to lower requirements to attract students; larger enrollments mean greater budgetary and personnel resources. Unfortunate and unwarranted competition among campuses could be the end result. To forestall this, systemwide monitoring and approval of campus undergraduate admission requirements will become an essential of system governance where it does not already exist. Unregulated enrollment competition should not become a substitute for the hard decisions of program and resource allocation which must be made. A lowering of admission or transfer requirements should not be permitted without assessing the possibilities of an increase in attrition rates, a need for increased remedial instruction, and the impact on other campuses within the system and on other public and private institutions.

These issues bring senior and community colleges into direct contact and possible conflict. Inevitable competition for students and programs will require continual review. Systemwide administration must defend the activities of senior colleges where appropriate and curtail them where not. Where not directly responsible for both segments, multicampus systems must recognize their interdependence with community colleges by cooperating in policies and programs which reflect a broader statewide interest.

The attraction of campuses, not central assignment of students, will determine the enrollment future for most institutions, and here there is much that can be accomplished. Indeed, the raison d'être for the multicampus system should be to increase the quality of campus programs in the face of tight resources, to attract students by promoting the qualities of diversity, specialization, and cooperation—the defining characteristics of the multicampus system.

Systemwide informational programs can aid students in locating campuses and programs most appropriate to their needs and talents. In an era of resource and program constraints, specialized curricula will be concentrated on particular campuses. This, in turn, may lead to the need for selected systemwide programs cutting across specialties and drawing upon the resources of the entire system. At the policy level, central leadership in the recognition and implementation of such opportunities would seem an essential response to the steady state. Procedurally, intercampus transfer programs can be expanded, and processing of admissions—whether campus-based or centralized —can be simplified to serve student needs.

Multicampus Systems in an Unsteady State

Writing in 1971, we concluded (p. 433): "The multicampus university can meet the challenges of the 1970s only if, in fact as in theory, it can develop as a system. More than in the past, the multicampus university must be greater than the sum of its parts." This challenge has been addressed. With a few exceptions, the increase in systemwide activity has been meritorious. Academic planning and program review are more comprehensive and of higher quality, budgeting is technically more sophisticated and more sensitive to academic criteria, multicampus programs are increasing, faculty personnel planning is being initiated, and student mobility is being facilitated. To be sure, few of these activities are limited to multicampus systems; indeed, the experiences of individual campuses, public and private, offer many lessons for systemwide administrators. But the record is sound. Multicampus systems have made a difference for students, for faculty, and for the educational enterprise of their states. The difference has been positive—more so, we believe, than would have been the case had the policies and decisions described in earlier chapters been the responsibility of single campuses, whether dealing with each other as autonomous institutions or dealing directly with state executive and legislative officials and with coordinating agencies.

We cannot compare the character and quality of higher education decision-making in states with and without multicampus systems. However, the record of the past five years supports the theory that many important policy decisions involving public higher education within a state can be more effectively resolved by an educational institution than by arms of state government. It is true that the central administration of a multicampus system is one step removed from the internal administration of campuses, but these are university systems, not state agencies, and differences between the two are profound.

Nowhere is this difference more apparent than in the fact that, in the face of pressures to centralize, multicampus systems have been unusually sensitive to the values of individual campuses. As often as not, increased systemwide activity has focused on improving the quality of campus decision-making, not on preempting judgments at the systemwide level. Thus, for example, decisions on program expansion or curtailment remain basically a campus prerogative, but one now informed by a wider understanding of systemwide resources, by systemwide stimulation of possibilities for regional coordination and cooperation, and by new guidelines and policies for evaluating program proposals. To the extent that campuses, single or in concert, can effectively shape their destiny, consistent with the wider needs of the system and the state, higher education is the better.

We would not deny the potential of a central administration iron hand within a velvet glove, a potential which at times must become a reality. Nor would we deny the existence of controversy over the appropriate role of the multicampus systemwide administration. Midway between state and campuses, system administrators are often the focus of the discontents of both. Campuses resent the time and effort the system requires of them so that it can be accountable to the state. The state, by the same token, is occasionally unhappy that system responsibility for campus autonomy prevents the direct intervention possible with other state agencies. In attempting to satisfy campuses and state, the multicampus system runs the very real risk of losing the backing of each. Yet it cannot exercise its governing and coordinating responsibilities in isolation. The support of both campus and state is essential, as suggested in these perceptive words of a leading system administrator:

> System administration lives in the vulnerable isolation
> of a no-man's-land, with little or no constituency on

which to build any credibility or support base. System administration tends to carry the black hat image with students, faculty, campus administrators and, perhaps, even campus alumni. . . . On the other hand, the system administrators, perceived to have powers of authority they have no way of exercising in an academic setting, are favorite political whipping boys for governors, legislators, and press playing political corners to gain favor with an always harrassed and unhappy taxpaying public. . . . Perhaps it is only paranoia showing through on the part of one who has now been engaged in system administration for many years. Nonetheless, I would state both to campus families and public officials, that if any of them are long to maintain the services of an effective system administration, it is in their own clear self-interest to show occasional concern for bolstering the credibility of the system administration rather than uniformly and consistently seeking to cast aspersions on it.

Multicampus systems are currently in midstream. The expansionist dreams of the 1960s have been left behind and the harsh reality of the 1980s lies ahead. But a major objective of multicampus administration has emerged from the experience of the past five years: for the foreseeable future, creative use must be made of the unique organizational structure that combines coordination and governance. Coordination implies a continuing high level of campus autonomy—the prerogative of the campuses to promote their own institutional stamp and style. Governance, on the other hand, implies that central administration has direct operational responsibility and is accountable to the state for the sum of activity across campuses. The tension between campus and central responsibility cannot be resolved by abandoning either. We believe we have shown that fiscal and enrollment pressures such as those expected over the coming decade need not inevitably lead to inappropriate centralization at the expense of desirable campus authority.

While the balance between centralization and campus authority will necessarily vary from system to system, an exemplary model would include the following:

Continuing and conscious awareness that most decisions, most of the time, are better made at campuses than centrally.
Equal awareness that some decisions—often the hardest ones – must be made by the central administration and the governing board.
The best possible information—historical, current, and projected —about programs and needs, coupled with judicious use of such information for more informed decisions at both campus and systemwide levels.
Flexibility within the multicampus system to employ budgetary resources effectively among campuses- and at the campus level, among programs—to ensure diversity and specialization in a period of increasing fiscal constraints.
Equitable procedures for dealing with personnel retrenchment, and positive programs of intercampus mobility to soften the impact of faculty layoffs.
Regional and systemwide academic programs which attract and engage the abilities of faculty and students beyond the horizons of a single campus.
Systemwide capacity—both technical and at the highest policy levels—for institutional self-analysis, evaluation, and change.
Ongoing efforts to mobilize energies of campus administrators, faculty, and students to seek solutions not only at their campuses but within the system as a whole.

Maintaining the balance between the system and the campuses will not be easy. Externally, state budgetary and coordinating agencies will be under pressure to intervene in system affairs. Internally, stability of staffing and—in some institutions —collective bargaining will harden traditional academic conservatism. Necessary flexibility at campus and system levels will be difficult to sustain, and controversy about which level should exercise it will abound. Nevertheless, the balance can be reached. Its achievement will define the success of multicampus systems in the unsteady state of the 1980s.

Questionnaire

In early 1974, an informal background questionnaire was sent to each system executive of nine multicampus universities. The questionnaire was not intended as an independent research instrument, but rather as a relatively structured way to identify changes in multicampus governance since our earlier study, to obtain opinions concerning the major impacts of enrollment stabilization and fiscal stringency, and to solicit predictions of changes expected to occur over the next five to ten years.

The 108 questions, spread over 72 typewritten pages, were divided among five reasonably discrete areas of inquiry: governance, faculty, admissions and transfers, academic programs, and budgeting. Although the questionnaire was addressed to the chief executive officer, it was suggested that staff responsible for these areas might answer the several parts of the questionnaire. This latter procedure was generally followed, although one chief executive personally completed the entire document. However, as subsequent interviews revealed, all system executives were knowledgeable about the questions and responses from their institution.

The questionnaire clearly served the purposes for which it was intended. As preparation for the interviews, it pinpointed overall issues to be covered across systems and specific questions for each of them. In addition, prior to the interviews, questionnaire results were furnished to system executives, both in the form of marginal aggregation and of a brief narrative summary of the highlights. Respondents were thus able to comment about their own institutions in the context of the nine systems as a whole, further enriching the interview process.

Representative questions and responses in each of the five areas are shown here only to indicate how the questionnaire assisted the study and to provide additional evidence to the discussion in the main text. It should be stressed, however, that many of the responses were both qualified and expanded upon in interviews and in the preparation and review of preliminary drafts. The responses should not be read in isolation but in the context of the full commentary presented above.

Governance

The relationship between a multicampus system with both governing and coordinating responsibilities and a statewide coordinating agency is troublesome in almost every state where the two coexist. Two of the questions concerning coordination asked about changes in the authority of coordinating agencies. These questions were not applicable to the Universities of North Carolina and Wisconsin, which had become single statewide governing boards since the earlier study. Although there was no general increase in authority of coordinating agencies during the past five years, no one perceived that it had decreased. However, an increase in coordinating authority is expected in the future by several institutions.

Since 1969, has there been any change in the review and/or de facto approval authority of the statewide coordinating agency over university activities?

	Change since 1969			Not Applicable
	Little or no change	Increase	Decrease	
a. New academic programs	5	2	—	—
b. Existing academic programs	5	2	—	—
c. Roles or missions of university campuses	5	2	—	—
d. Funding priorities for university campuses	6	1	—	—
e. Faculty salary levels	7	—	—	—

	Change since 1969			Not
	Little or no change	*Increase*	*Decrease*	*Not Applicable*
f. Tuition	6	—	—	1
g. Admissions policy	6	1	—	—
h. Other	2	—	—	—

What changes, if any, do you expect in the level of review and/or de facto approval authority of the statewide coordinating agency over university activities?

	1979	1984
a. Little or no change from present	3	2
b. Coordinating agency's role will *increase*	4	2+ "?"
c. Coordinating agency's role will *decrease*		1

A major development in academic governance is, of course, the emergence of faculty collective bargaining as an issue. This was reflected in the following responses. Although there is only occasional faculty interest at present, all but one system predicts an increase in activity by 1979.

Which of the following best describes your perception of faculty interest in collective bargaining activity in your system?

a. __3__ Little or no interest at any campus
b. __1__ Some interest by all faculty at all campuses
c. __2__ Substantial interest by all faculty at all campuses
d. __2__ Interest varies by campus
e. __1__ Other

What is your expectation of change in faculty collective bargaining activity in the short run (1979)? In the long run (1984)?

	1979	1984
a. Little or no change	1	—
b. Activity will *increase*	8	7+ "?"
c. Activity will *decrease*	—	1

Faculty

One possible strategy for meeting differential enrollment trends among campuses within a system would entail the permanent or temporary transfer of faculty among campuses. Responses to two of the questions concerning this possibility indicated that, despite little change in policy since the earlier study, it is an area in which change is expected in the future.

Since 1969, what changes, if any, have taken place in universitywide policy towards permanent and temporary transfers of faculty among its campuses?

	Permanent transfers	Temporary transfers (one year or less)
a. Little or no change	8	5
b. Transfers are encouraged *more* now than they were in 1969	1	4
c. Transfers are encouraged *less* now than they were in 1969	—	—

What changes do you expect in university policy on faculty transfers among its campuses in the short run (1979)? In the long run (1984)?

	1979	1984
a. Permanent transfers		
(1) Little or no change from present	2+ "?"	2+ "?"
(2) *More* encouragement	6	6
(3) *Less* encouragement	—	—
b. Temporary transfers (one year or less)		
(1) Little or no change from present	3	3
(2) *More* encouragement	6	6
(3) *Less* encouragement	—	—

Also in the area of faculty affairs, the unanimity of responses to one question clearly points to the existence of a major steady state problem.

On any of its campuses, does the university now or in the foreseeable future face the problem of lack of faculty "new blood"—that is, insufficient vacancies because of unequal distribution by rank or age?

                        9   —
                       Yes No

Admissions and Transfers

It might be expected that as enrollment stabilizes, a multicampus system would increase its control over campus admissions policies. However, only two respondents indicated that this has occurred or predicted that such control would increase in the future. (Despite these responses, based on subsequent interviews, we predict an increase in systemwide surveillance—and probably control—in most systems.)

Since 1969, have any changes taken place in universitywide control over campus admission policies?

	No change	*Less control*	*More control*	*Not applicable*
a. Freshman admissions	7	—	2	—
b. Graduate admissions other than law and medicine	9	—	—	—
c. Admission to law and medical schools	7	—	1	1
d. Admission of transfer student from two-year colleges	6	—	3	—

What changes, if any, do you expect in universitywide control over campus admissions policies in the short run (1979)?

	1979			
	No change	*Less control*	*More control*	*Not applicable*
a. Freshman admissions	8	—	1	—
b. Graduate admissions other than law and medicine	8	—	1	—
c. Admission to law and medical schools	6	—	2	1
d. Admissions of transfer students from two-year colleges	8	—	1	—

What changes, if any, do you expect in universitywide control over campus admissions policies in the long run (1984)?

	1984			
	No change	*Less control*	*More control*	*Not applicable*
a. Freshman admissions	7	—	2	—
b. Graduate admissions other than law and medicine	8	—	1	—
c. Admissions to law and medical schools	7	—	1	1
d. Admission of transfer students from two-year colleges	8	—	1	—

With respect to intercampus student transfers, important changes have apparently taken place and are expected. Reportedly, it is now easier for students to transfer among campuses of a system than in the past, and further liberalization is expected.

Since 1969, what change, if any, has there been in universitywide policy regarding the permanent transfer of students *among its campuses* and the temporary or joint enrollment of such students (e.g., for enrollment in a single course, for a single semester, etc.)?

	Permanent transfer	Temporary transfer or joint enrollment for a limited time or purpose
a. Little or no change	2	2
b. *Easier* for a student to transfer or jointly enroll now than in 1969	6	6
c. *More difficult* for a student to transfer or jointly enroll now than in 1969	—	—
d. Other	1	1

What changes, if any, do you expect in the ease or difficulty of students moving *among university campuses* to use the resources of another campus on either a permanent or a temporary basis in the short run (1979)? In the long run (1984)?

	1979	1984
a. Little or no change	2	2
b. Student movement will be *easier*	6	6
c. Student movement will become *more difficult*	—	—
d. Other	1	1

Academic Programs

Almost half of the questionnaire concerned differing aspects of academic plans and programs, for example, the expected usefulness of systemwide academic plans.

What changes do you expect in the usefulness of formal, long range or medium range academic plans for the university in the short run (1979)? In the long run (1984)?

	1979	1984
a. No change	2	1
b. Substantially *more* useful than at the present time	6	7
c. Substantially *less* useful than at the present time	1	1

A single exception was noted to the general expectation that academic plans will be either more useful over the coming decade; in one system, it is expected that state governmental and coordinating agencies will be under pressure to interfere with (and undercut the effectiveness of) orderly university planning processes as enrollment and funding stabilize.

The responses to questions about systemwide review of new and existing academic programs clearly emphasized the recent and expected change in this area of academic affairs. In the past five years, systemwide review of new programs has become more stringent, and the trend is expected to continue.

Since 1969, what changes have taken place in universitywide review of *new* academic programs?

a. __6__ More *inclusive* now than in 1969—i.e., encompassing more programs or courses
b. __7__ More stringent now than in 1969 based on *academic quality*
c. __6__ More stringent now than in 1969 based on *campus mission*, role, or scope criteria
d. __8__ More stringent now than in 1969 based on *fiscal* criteria
e. __1__ Other

What changes do you expect in the inclusiveness and/or stringency of universitywide review of *new* academic programs in the short run (1979)? In the long run (1984)?

	1979	1984
a. Little or no change	2	1
b. Review will be *more* inclusive and/or *more* stringent	6	7
c. Review will be *less* inclusive and/or *less* stringent	—	—
d. Other	1	1

Similarly, with respect to existing academic programs, review has generally been established within the past five years, and is expected to become increasingly comprehensive and stringent in the future.

How long have current universitywide procedures, if any, for periodic review of *existing* academic programs been in effect?

	None in effect	In effect		
		Less than 5 years	5 to 10 years	More than 10 years
a. Existing undergraduate programs	3	5	—	1
b. Existing graduate and professional programs	1	7	—	1

What changes do you expect in universitywide review of *existing* academic programs in the short run (1979)? In the long run (1984)?

	1979	1984
a. Little or no change	1	1
b. Review will be *more* inclusive and/or *more* stringent	7	7
c. Review will be *less* inclusive and/or *less* stringent	—	—
d. Other	1	1

Responses to questions concerning new or innovative methods of instruction reveal a unanimous expectation that interest in these will increase. On the other hand, while factors thought to encourage or discourage such programs in the past were identified, few of these seem to make very much difference.

What changes do you expect in universitywide interest in innovation and experimentation with instructional programs in the short run (1979)? In the long run (1984)?

	1979	1984
a. Little or no change	—	—
b. Universitywide interest will *increase*	9	9
c. Universitywide interest will *decrease*	—	—

Since 1969, have the following encouraged or discouraged universitywide efforts to institute and assess new or innovative methods of instruction— e.g., nontraditional studies, televised instruction, etc.?

	Encouraged		No Impact	Discouraged	
	Some	Very much	No Impact	Some	Very much
a. Faculty interest or lack of it in change from tradition	6	1	—	5	—
b. Student interest or lack of it in new programs	7	2	—	—	—
c. Adequacy or inadequacy of state funding level	1	—	2	5	2
d. Flexibility or inflexibility of state budgetary practices	—	—	3	5	1
e. Public opinion	6	1	2	1	—
f. Extramural funding	7	2	—	—	—
g. Interest or lack of it by campus administrators	7	2	—	—	—
h. State legislative pressures	3	—	4	2	—
i. Other	1	—	—	—	—

Systemwide academic programs, a potential source of cooperative activity in the steady state, are in place and expected to increase in the next five to ten years.

Are there any degree programs in the university which have been specifically designed to require, involve, or encourage academic work at two or more campuses?

8	1
Yes	No

What changes do you expect in universitywide academic programs and activities in the short run (1979)? In the long run (1984)?

	1979	1984
a. Little or no change from present	—	—
b. Universitywide academic programs and activities will *increase*	9	9
c. Universitywide academic programs and activities will *decrease*	—	—

Budgeting

As revealed in subsequent interviews, sections of the questionnaire dealing with budgeting failed to identify growing relationships between system budgeting practices and academic planning and program review. In part, too, wide differences in state
budgeting procedure make it difficult to obtain responses on a
comparable basis. Nevertheless, the following generalizations
from the responses deserve mention.

State agency review of systemwide (as opposed to campus)
budgets has become more detailed since 1969 and is expected
to increase in the future.

Since 1969, has state agency review of the details of university and/or
campus budgets increased or decreased?

	Campus	*Universitywide*
a. Little or no change since 1969	2	1
b. *More* details are reviewed now than in 1969	4	7
c. *Less* details are reviewed now than in 1969	3	1

What changes do you expect in the concern of state agencies with the details of budget requests in the short run (1979)? In the long run (1984)?

	1979	*1984*
a. Little or no change	—	—
b. *More* concern with the details of budget requests	7	5
c. *Less* concern with the details of budget requests	1	3
d. Other	1	1

Similarly, legislative and gubernatorial interest in various
aspects of budgeting has tended to have an impact upon internal
university management.

Since 1969, how, if at all, have the following aspects of budgeting limited
the university and its campuses in managing academic programs?

	Little or not at all	*Some-what*	*Very much*	*Not applicable*
a. Legislative or gubernatorial interest in specific programs	2	6	1	—
b. Legislative or gubernatorial interest in specific campuses	4	4	1	—

	Little or not at all	Some- what	Very much	Not applicable
c. Restrictions over transfer of funds among line items or other appropriation categories	5	2	1	1
d. Budget bill control language regulating expenditures for specific programs or campuses	2	5	2	—
e. Conference committee or other expression of legislative intent regulating specific programs or campuses	2	6	1	—
f. Campus pressure for equal treatment	5	3	1	—
g. Faculty collective bargaining agreements	2	—	1	6

Finally, although four of the systems report new sources of fiscal flexibility since 1969 (e.g., student fees), the institutions have also experienced decreases in flexibility in specific areas.

Does the university now have any sources for university-wide fiscal flexibility that it did not have in 1969?	4 Yes 5 No

Since 1969, have any of the following factors (considering each separately) increased or decreased in value as a source of flexibility to the university in budget administration?

	Increased	Decreased	Little or no change	Not applicable
a. Expressly appropriated contingency funds	1	2	2	4
b. Federal indirect cost reimbursement	2	3	3	1
c. Extramural grants and contracts	—	1	7	1
d. Current gifts	—	—	8	1
e. Cost or salary savings	2	4	2	1
f. Income from endowment	1	—	7	1
g. Student fees	3	1	5	—

	Increased	Decreased	Little or no change	Not applicable
h. Retention of portion of campus appropriation in universitywide pool for subsequent allocation	5	2	1	1

References

American Association of University Professors. *Revision of Regulation 4, Recommended Institutional Regulations on Academic Freedom and Tenure.* Washington, D.C., 1974.

Boulding, K. E. *The Management of Decline.* Address to the Regents Convocation of the University of the State of New York. Albany, 1974.

Breneman, D. W. "Predicting the Response of Graduate Education to No Growth." *New Directions for Institutional Research,* 1975, No. 6, 77-87.

California State University and Colleges. *Institutional Research Memorandum.* Los Angeles, Feb. 1968.

California State University and Colleges. *Memorandum IR 73-36.* Los Angeles, Nov. 1973a.

California State University and Colleges. *Program for Innovation.* Los Angeles, 1973b.

California State University and Colleges. *Trustees Agenda Item 2.* Los Angeles, Nov. 1973c.

California State University and Colleges. *Academic Program and Resource Planning in the California State University and Colleges, 1974-75 Through 1978-79.* Los Angeles, April 1974a.

California State University and Colleges. *Institutional Research Memorandum.* Los Angeles, July 1974b.

California State University and Colleges. *Institutional Research Memorandum.* Los Angeles, Aug. 1974c.

California State University and Colleges. *Report from Task Force on Steady State Staffing.* Los Angeles, Nov. 1974d.

California State University and Colleges. *Statistical Abstract of the California State University and Colleges, 1973.* Los Angeles, 1974e.

Carlson, D., and Gordon, M. S. *Enrollment Projections for Higher Education to the Year 2000.* San Francisco: Jossey-Bass, 1975.

Carnegie Commission on Higher Education. *The More Effective Use of Resources.* New York: McGraw-Hill, 1972.

Carnegie Foundation for the Advancement of Teaching. *More Than Survival.* San Francisco: Jossey-Bass, 1975.

City University of New York. *1972 Master Plan of the Board of Higher Education of the City University of New York.* New York, July 1972.

City University of New York. *The Evaluation of CUNY Colleges.* New York, 1974a.

City University of New York. *Freshman Allocations.* Memorandum from J. Joseph Meng to members of the Committee on Administrative Affairs. New York, May 1974b.

City University of New York. *Memorandum.* From Mary P. Bass and David Newton to college presidents. New York, May 1974c.

City University of New York. *The 1974 Progress Report of the Board of Higher Education for the City University of New York.* New York, June 1974d.

Commission on Academic Tenure in Higher Education. *Faculty Tenure.* San Francisco: Jossey-Bass, 1973.

Coordinating Board, Texas College and University System. *Public Senior College Development in Texas to 1980.* Austin, 1968.

Enarson, H. L. "University or Knowledge Factory." *The Chronicle of Higher Education,* June 18, 1973, p. 16.

Gardner, J. W. "Universities as Designers of the Future." *Educational Record,* Fall 1967, *48,* 315-319.

Glenny, L. A., and others. *Presidents Confront Reality.* San Francisco: Jossey-Bass, 1975.

Henry, D. *Challenges Past, Challenges Present: A Critical Look at American Higher Education Since 1930.* San Francisco: Jossey-Bass, 1975.

Hollander, T. E. *Curiouser and Curiouser.* Statement before the Executive Committee of the Association of Colleges and Universities of New York. Rensselaerville, June 1974.

Illinois Board of Higher Education. *A Master Plan—Phase III for Higher Education in Illinois.* Springfield, May 1971.

Johnson v. Regents, United States District Court, Western District, Wisconsin, 1974.

Lanier, L. H. "Comment on 'Statewide Reallocation through Program Priorities.' " *Educational Record,* Summer 1973, *54,* 184-190.

Lee, E. C., and Bowen, F. M. *The Multicampus University.* New York: McGraw-Hill, 1971.

Newman, F., and others. *Report on Higher Education.* Washington, D.C.: U.S. Office of Education, 1971.

New York State Education Department. *Meeting the Needs of Doctoral Education.* Albany, August 1973.

"Opening Fall Enrollments 1972, 1973, and 1974." *The Chronicle of Higher Education,* December 16, 1974.

State of California. *1974 Budget Bill.* Sacramento, 1974a.

State of California. *Request for Proposal of Joint Committee on Postsecondary Education.* Sacramento, June 1974b.

State of California. *Supplementary Report of the Committee on Conference.* Legislative Analyst's Report. Sacramento, June 1974c.

State of New York. *Governor's Budget, 1974-75.* Albany, 1974a.

State of New York. *Legislative Press Release on 1974-75 State Budget.* Albany, 1974b.

State of North Carolina Board of Higher Education. *Planning for Higher Education in North Carolina.* Raleigh, 1968.

State of Wisconsin. *Letter.* Governor Patrick J. Lucey to Frank J. Pelisek, President, University of Wisconsin Board of Regents. Madison, January 8, 1975.

State University of New York. *Guidelines for Evaluation of Graduate Programs.* Albany, November 1972a.

State University of New York. *Reaffirmation and Reform, the 1972 Master Plan of the State University of New York.* Albany, 1972b.

State University of New York. *Campus-Central Staff Relationships.* Albany, 1973.

State University of New York. *Letter.* From President McGrath accompanying "Report of the Committee on Academic Priorities." Binghamton, February 1974a.

State University of New York. *1974 Progress Report.* Albany, June, 1974b.

"Statewide Planning vs. University Autonomy." *The Chronicle of Higher Education,* January 27, 1975, p. 7.

University of California. *Ten Year Enrollment Projections.* Berkeley, April 1969.

University of California. *University Bulletin.* Berkeley, August 1970.

University of California. *Memorandum.* President to chancellors. Berkeley, June 1972.

University of California. *The Extended University: A Progress Report.* Berkeley, 1974a.

University of California. *Memorandum.* C. O. McCorkle Jr. to Albert Bowker. Berkeley, April 1974b.

University of California. *Memorandum.* President Hitch to chancellors. Berkeley, April 1974c.

University of California. *Toward Excellence in Teaching, Too- A Study of the Special $1 Million Fund for Improvement of Undergraduate Instruction in the University of California.* Berkeley, October 1974d.

University of California. *University of California Academic Plan, 1974-1978.* Berkeley, March 1974e.

University of California. *University of California Analysis of the Budget for Current Operations and Capital Improvements.* Berkeley, October 1974f.

University of California. *Educational Objectives for the University of California.* Report of the Academic Senate Committee on Long Range Educational Objectives and Academic Planning. Berkeley, 1975a.

University of California. *University of California Academic Plan, Phase II.* Volume I: The Universitywide Perspective. Berkeley, March, 1975b.

University of Illinois. *Provisional Development Plan, 1971-72 Through 1980-81.* Urbana, September 1970.

University of Illinois. *Scope and Mission of the University of Illinois, 1974-1980.* Urbana, May 1974.

University of Missouri. *On Campus Enrollment Projections.* Columbia, April 1970.

University of Missouri. *Memorandum.* Vice president for academic affairs to Kerley, and others. Columbia, August 1973a.

University of Missouri. *Numbers of Intercampus Transfers Academic Year 1972-73.* Columbia, April 1973b.

University of Missouri. *President's Bulletin.* Columbia, February 1973c.

University of Missouri. *Enrollment Projections for the University of Missouri, 1974 to 1978.* Columbia, May 1974a.

University of Missouri. *The University of Missouri Academic Plan 1975-85.* Part I: Degree Programs. Columbia, September 1974b.

University of North Carolina. *The Code of the Board of Governors of the University of North Carolina.* Chapel Hill, September 1973.

University of North Carolina. *Administrative Memorandum No. 27.* Chapel Hill, January 1974a.

University of North Carolina. *Administrative Memorandum No. 33.* Chapel Hill, April 1974b.

University of North Carolina. *Letter.* President Friday to Peter Holmes. Chapel Hill, June 1974c.

University of North Carolina. *Statistical Abstract of Higher Education in North Carolina, 1973-74.* Chapel Hill, 1974d.

University of Texas. *Report of the Visiting Committee for the Evaluation of the Joint Ph.D. Program in Mathematical Sciences.* Arlington and Dallas, undated.

University of Texas. *Austin Faculty Minutes.* Austin, January 1974a.

University of Texas. *Enrollment Projections, 1974-1980.* Austin, 1974b.

University of Texas. *Precis of the Academic Plan, the University of Texas at Dallas.* Dallas, 1974c.

University of Wisconsin. *Enrollment Projections, University of Wisconsin System, 1975 through 1982.* Madison, 1973a.

University of Wisconsin. *Memorandum.* Senior vice president to chancellors. Madison, November 1973b.

University of Wisconsin. *Memorandum.* Senior vice president to task force. Madison, November 1973c.

University of Wisconsin. *Fee Experiment at Fond du Lac and Rice Lake.* Memorandum from President Weaver to Regents. Madison, January 1974a.

University of Wisconsin. *Mission.* Madison, 1974b.

University of Wisconsin. *1975-77 Biennial Operating Budget Policy Paper #2.0.* Madison, September 1974c.

University of Wisconsin. *Planning Principles.* Draft revision. Madison, 1974d.

University of Wisconsin. *Report to Education Committee, Board of Regents.* Madison, January 1974e.

University of Wisconsin. *President's Report in Response to the Governor's Request on Reducing the Scope of the University of Wisconsin System.* Madison, April 1975.

Wisconsin Coordinating Council on Higher Education. *Publication 70-1.* Madison, 1970.

Index

31-32, 33-34; academic planning and program review board of, 52-53; admission policy of, 120; affirmative action at, 75; at Berkeley, 7, 33, 119, 122, 123, 125-126, 131; budgeting for, 60-61, 63, 64-65, 66, 71, 73, 75; campus-based reviews at, 48; community college relationships of, 129; context and governance of, 7-8; at Davis, 7, 108, 126; enrollment at, 7-8, 60-61, 63, 64-65, 103, 119; existing programs reviewed at, 48, 52-53; Extended University of, 80-81; faculty organization at, 18; faculty retrenchment at, 99, 102-104, 110, 116, 117; faculty specialization at, 108; financial distress of, 5, 8; fiscal flexibility at, 66, 71, 73; governing board of, 17; innovation at, 96; at Irvine, 8, 34; at Los Angeles, 7, 33, 75, 122; new programs reviewed at, 41; nontraditional programs at, 79, 80-81, 84; physical facilities of, 33-34; program development at, 79, 80-81, 88, 96; program review at, 37-38, 39, 41, 48, 52-53; redirection of students by, 33-34, 125-126; retirement from, 117; at Riverside, 8, 33-34, 103, 119, 123; at San Diego, 7, 34; at Santa Barbara, 7, 8; at Santa Cruz, 7, 8, 116; selective, system-based program review at, 52-53; specificity of plans for, 31-32; state intervention in budgeting for, 75; systemwide programs of, 88; tenure at, 110; tenure impaction at, 116; transfer of students at, 130; at Ventura Learning Center, 83

Carlson, D., xi*n*, 163

Carnegie Commission on Higher Education, 109, 163

Carnegie Corporation, 72, 94

Carnegie Council on Policy Studies in Higher Education, xv

Carnegie Foundation for the Advancement of Teaching, xi, 3, 163

Center for Research and Development in Higher Education, 121

Change, intentional, 132-133

Citizens' commission, for academic planning in New York, 24

City University of New York. *See* New York, City University of

Collective bargaining, and fiscal flexibility, 72-73

Commission on Academic Tenure in Higher Education, 109-110, 113, 164

Community colleges, relationships of, with senior colleges, 127-129, 145

Coordinating agencies, governance by, 16

Corbally, J., xiv

D

Dumke, G., xiv

E

Enarson, H. L., 18-19, 164

Enrollment: admissions related to, 119; and budgeting, 60-65; complexity of, 62-65; and faculty, 98-107; and nontraditional programs, 84; rate of, 2-3; timing of, 60-62; in universities, 5

Executive agencies, governance by, 15

External degree programs, 79-84

F

Facilities, physical, academic planning influenced by, 33-35

Faculty: adjustment of number of, 99; and enrollment, 98-107; governance by, 17-18; procedures for layoff of, 99-107, 112-114, 142; renewal of, 143; retirement plans for, 117, 144; retrenchment strategies for, 97-117, 141-144, 153-154; salaries of, and inflation, 114-115, 144; specialization of, and curricular change, 108-109; tenured, systemwide or campus-based, 109-112, 143; and tenure impaction, 116-117, 144, 154

Fiscal flexibility: and academic budgeting, 65-73; and collective bargaining, 72-73; through discretionary funds, 68-70; through grants, 71-72; through indirect cost reimbursement, 70-71; through reallocation of funds, 66-67; state administrators and, 67-68; through transfer of funds, 65-66

Fiscal stringency, review of new programs influenced by, 39-42

Fleming Commission, 40

Ford Foundation, 72

Friday, W., xiv

Fynmore, D., xiv

G

Gardner, J. W., 132, 164

Glenny, L. A., xi*n*, 121, 164